HEAVY ARTILLERY OF WWII

TERRY GANDER

Airlife

Copyright © 2004 The Crowood Press Ltd

Text written by Terry Gander

First published in the UK in 2004
by Airlife Publishing Ltd, an imprint of The Crowood Press

British Library Cataloguing-in-Publication Data
A catalogue record for this book
is available from the British Library

ISBN 1 84037 414 4

Printed in China

For a complete list of all Airlife titles please contact:

Airlife

An imprint of The Crowood Press
Ramsbury, Marlborough, Wiltshire SN8 2HR
E-mail: enquiries@crowood.com

www.crowood.com

Foreword

When considering the heavy artillery employed during World War II one of the main initial conclusions reached is that the term 'heavy artillery' varied widely from nation to nation. For some national armies, heavy artillery calibres started at just over 105mm. For others the term began to be applied at about 150mm. To confuse matters, post-1950 developments reclassified many of the lighter calibres included in these pages as 'medium'. There was never any limit above those calibres, although for some the term 'super-heavy artillery' was used, although usually in a journalistic sense. We will consider those pieces with calibres above 105mm in service between 1939 and 1945. Railway artillery is not included.

A second conclusion that will soon be reached is that most of the heavy artillery pieces deployed between 1939 and 1945 were almost in the antique class. In fact the vast bulk of them dated from the Great War years of 1914–18, if not before. This situation was largely brought about by the widespread political belief that the Treaty of Versailles marked the end of the war that ended all wars. Some nations had never accepted this, yet it took nearly 20 years for general opinion to change. Those 20 years witnessed a general dearth of artillery development in all calibres, with the expensive development of heavy artillery being the most affected, as there seemed to be little use for such military luxuries.

Heavy artillery forms an expensive military commodity, in terms of finance and other resources. For many pieces the term 'heavy' related not just to the projectile fired, but to the corresponding guns and howitzers involved in delivering them. Some of the pieces deployed during both World Wars were heavy to excess. Moving them was a ponderous undertaking that took time and a great deal of effort. During the then-accepted conventional mode of warfare, which involved manoeuvre on a grand scale, heavy artillery rarely got a chance to become involved, other than during siege warfare, when the time factor was usually not critical to operations. In 1914 it was anticipated that mobile warfare would be the norm, so heavy artillery was not widely issued on anything other than a token scale. But by the end of 1914 that had all changed.

The Western Front trenches soon settled into a routine close to siege warfare, so the call went out for heavy artillery to blast a way through the field fortification lines that became established on a grand scale. It was produced at great cost and diversion of resources, usually in a rush. That rush dictated that there was rarely time for engineering finesse to be applied to what were usually huge and heavy artillery pieces that needed time and labour to install, had a slow rate of fire, and demanded large teams of gunners to service and move them.

After 1918 those heavy pieces had to be retained. There was no sense in scrapping them, no matter that no more wars were expected. During the inter-war years they were rarely fired, or even taken from their gun sheds, so in 1939 they were put back into active service. But there were two important national exceptions.

They were Germany and the Soviet Union. The German army had to be built up again almost from scratch during the 1920s and 1930s, as the terms imposed by the Versailles Treaty forbade the nation to even own heavy artillery. The Soviet Union was in a similar situation, although their dearth of almost all types of military matériel was imposed by the upheavals of the post-1918 Civil War period and the general disruption of the manufacturing infrastructure left from the Tsarist era. Both Germany and the Soviet Union were therefore in a position to capitalise on the latest state-of-the-art artillery innovations derived from advances in metallurgy, chemical engineering and many other associated topics. It was therefore possible for both states to design, develop and manufacture modern heavy artillery with many of the shortcomings of its forebears eliminated, or at least reduced. The 'new' heavy artillery was less cumbersome, had greater potential range and was more mobile, the increased mobility attributable largely to the introduction of motorised traction to replace the huge horse teams that had once been necessary.

Some inter-war heavy artillery development was undertaken in France, Italy and the UK. The USA also laid plans but, as in Europe, the economic climate there was such that few plans could reach the hardware stage in time for World War II. By 1940 heavy artillery was once again being given the attention it deserved, but at first the veterans were all that was to hand. The Battle of France in 1940 demonstrated that artillery power was still an important war weapon, even under the highly mobile conditions imposed by German armour. Thereafter, its power and numbers increased in leaps and bounds to ensure it remained 'The Last Argument of Kings'. That is, until the aircraft and the tank eventually became its equals in terms of battlefield dominance.

Belgium
Canon de 120 L mle 1931

During the 1920s the wealth produced by the largest of Belgium's colonies, the Belgian Congo, was such that the Belgian army was in a good position to renovate what was left of its 1914–18 artillery park. Belgium had received numbers of ex-German 75mm field guns as part of a package of post-1918 war reparations, and it was decided to update them while adding a heavier piece to provide extra artillery firepower to augment the relatively short-ranged 155mm (5.9in) howitzers then in service. The result was the Canon de 120 L mle 1931, produced by the Société Anonyme John Cockerill of Liège. As the designation implies, the first example was accepted by the Belgian army during 1931. Thereafter production was slow, for by 1939 there were only 24 in service. German lists mention 38 by the time they invaded Belgium.

The 120mm (4.72in) mle 1931 ordnance, 37 calibres long, was a sound, conventional design with a vertical sliding breech. It was placed on an all-steel, box-section, split-trail carriage to provide a wide angle of traverse once emplaced. The carriage's stability was greatly enhanced during firing by trail pad assemblies held securely in position by a series of metal stakes hammered into the ground. Many observers of the time considered that the mle 1931 fired a useful 21.93kg (48.35lb) high-explosive projectile. They also considered that the maximum range, 17,500m (19,145yd), was also commendable, although the prolonged rate of fire of a single round per minute after only a few rounds had been fired was perhaps too slow for a piece of its calibre, while the travelling weight (5,800kg/12,789lb) was a bit on the heavy side. The gun had to be towed by an FN-Kégresse half-tracked tractor unit produced specifically for the purpose.

In 1940 almost all of the Belgians' artillery holdings fell into German hands. They considered the mle 1931 was good enough to be retained for their own purposes, so they gave it a new designation, that of 12cm Kanone 370(b). As far as can be determined, none of these captured guns were deployed with field units within occupied Belgium, as all survivors were deployed for coastal or beach defence in prepared concrete ring emplacements along the Atlantic Wall, extending as far north as Norway. Only one example seems to have survived the fortunes of war after 1945, and it now resides in the Brussels War Museum.

Specification		
Calibre:	120mm	4.72in
Length of piece:	4.426m	174.25in
Weight travelling:	5,800kg	12,789lb
Weight in action:	5,450kg	12,017lb
Traverse:	60°	
Elevation:	0 to +38°30'	
Muzzle velocity:	760m/s	2,494ft/sec
Max range:	17,500m	19,145yd
Shell weight:	21.93kg	48.35lb

A Canon de 120 L mle 1931 on display in Belgium

Czechoslovakia
Skoda 149mm Model 28 (NOa) Gun

In several ways the Skoda 149mm Model 28 (NOa) gun was a throw-back to a previous era, as it was an export model of the type of long-range gun Skoda had been adept at manufacturing prior to 1918. It was a statically emplaced gun intended to deliver fire to targets such as fortifications while perhaps doubling as a coastal defence weapon, for it had to be fired from a heavy, prefabricated, steel ground platform located on a prepared site. Even by 1928 there can have been few applications for such a gun, other than siege or trench warfare. Any moves were carried out by dividing the gun into three main loads; barrel, cradle and platform, all carried on special transport trailers. A fourth load was made up from tools, handling equipment, sights and so on. Ammunition was carried separately on trucks. The weights involved meant that mechanical traction was essential but travelling during moves was slow.

When emplaced, after considerable labour, even with handling devices such as collapsible cranes, the Model 28 had the advantage of a full 360° traverse and the ability to fire a 56kg (123.5lb) high-explosive projectile to a range of 23,800m (26,037yd). The rate of fire was limited to one round a minute, at best, for between firings the barrel had to be lowered to the minimum elevation angle of +6° for loading. Delayed-action fuzes were available for when firing against armoured targets to allow the projectile to penetrate before detonating. The barrel was 46.5 calibres long. The 149mm Model 28 (NOa) was not considered for the Czechoslovak army, all output being directed to exports as a package combined with the 220mm (8.66in) Model 28 (ONa) howitzer (qv) – the two shared the same platform and cradle.

Two nations are recorded as customers for the gun. One was Romania, but no record has been found of the quantities involved and any subsequent employment by them. The other customer was Yugoslavia, where the guns were intended to provide the main striking power of the artillery. About 20 guns were involved. Their static nature meant they had little part to play during the rapid German occupation of 1941, and thereafter the guns became German property. Exactly what they did with them is uncertain, although some references mention service on the Eastern Front. They were given the German designation of 15cm K 403(j).

The Skoda 149mm Model 28 (NOa) gun ready to fire

Specification		
Calibre:	149.1mm	5.87in
Length of piece:	7,025mm	276.6in
Weight travelling (total):	39,800kg	87,742lb
Weight in action (approx):	15,000kg	33,075lb
Traverse:	360°	
Elevation:	+6 to +45°	
Muzzle velocity:	820m/s	2,690ft/sec
Max range:	23,800m	26,037yd
Shell weight:	56kg	123.5lb

The carriage of the Skoda 149mm Model 28 (NOa) gun on its special transporter

Czechoslovakia
Skoda 152mm Model 15/16 Gun

The origins of the Skoda 152mm Model 15/16 gun could be traced back to before 1914 when the old Austro-Hungarian army finally decided to replace a heavy gun dating from 1880. Development of the new gun by Skoda was rather protracted, for the first example, the 152mm Model 15, was not accepted until 1915. The gun emerged as a large, rather awkward-looking, cumbersome beast that had to be transported in two loads, barrel and carriage, even though the gun was designed from the outset as an 'Autokanone' to be towed by special wheeled tractors.

It fired a useful 54kg (119lb) projectile to a good range. That range was later increased to 21,840m (23,893yd) by alterations to the carriage that increased the maximum elevation angle from +32° to +45°, resulting in the Model 15/16. Only 27 examples of the Model 15 were completed before the elevation change was introduced. Production totals for the Model 15/16 have not been found recorded, but must have been significant, for it became one of the standard heavy guns of the post-1918 Austrian and Czechoslovak armies, although by 1938 the Austrian guns had long been withdrawn from service (one can still be seen in the Vienna Arsenal).

By 1939 only a few Czech guns remained as reserves, yet they were serviceable enough to be taken over by the German army to be utilised within the Atlantic Wall defences as the 15.2cm K 15/16(t).

This was despite their rate of fire of just one round a minute and limited on-carriage traverse. After 1918 the Model 15/16 also became a favoured Italian army weapon, either through capture or from war reparations. By June 1940 there were still 29 in service, known as the Cannone da 152/37, the '37' denoting the approximate length of the barrel. The Italian guns saw active service in Albania, Greece and North Africa. By the end of 1940 only 21 serviceable examples were left, all but four of them based in Italy, and some of those had been installed as coastal defence guns. During the 1920s the Italian guns had been extensively refurbished by Vickers-Terni and provided with new barrel liners, chambers and revised wheels. Any that were still in service when the Germans took over Italy during 1943 became the 15.2cm K 410(i). The Germans appear to have made little use of their Italian trophies.

Specification		
Calibre:	152.4mm	6in
Length of piece:	6,000mm	236.25in
Weight travelling (total):	16,415kg	36,188lb
Weight in action (approx):	11,900kg	26,240lb
Traverse:	6°	
Elevation:	-6 to +45°	
Muzzle velocity:	700m/s	2,297ft/sec
Max range:	21,840m	23,893yd
Shell weight:	54kg	119lb

The imposing bulk of a Skoda 152mm Model 15/16 gun

The barrel assembly (left) and the carriage (right) of the Skoda 152mm Model 15/16 gun

Czechoslovakia
Skoda 210mm K52 Gun Series

The 1919 Treaty of Versailles precluded the German Krupp concern from manufacturing heavy artillery, so when Turkey, hitherto an avid Krupp customer, was seeking to modernise its heavy-artillery holdings during the 1930s it turned to Skoda. Working to Turkish specifications, Skoda used the design designation of 'XV' to develop a powerful long-range gun that came into production in early 1939 as the 210mm K52. Only two examples were delivered to Turkey before Germany marched into Czechoslovakia and the uncompleted

guns became German property – the Turks never did receive any further guns.

By March 1940 German ordnance personnel had decided to maintain the K52 line in production for their own purposes. The K52 thus became the 21cm K 39 and from then on could be regarded as a German product from what had become the Waffenfabrik Pilsen. Ten examples of the K 39 were completed, using already-manufactured components, before German technicians introduced measures to simplify production, and provision for a muzzle

A recognition illustration from an Allied manual showing a 210mm K52 gun while on the move

A German-owned 21cm K 39 in action – the Skoda 210mm K52

brake was added, making the revised gun, the 21cm K 39/40, the largest German artillery piece provided with such a device. The muzzle brake enabled German-designed heavier propellant charges and projectiles to be employed, increasing the maximum range to 34,000m (37,183yd) without imposing undue stresses on the carriage. Twenty examples of the K 39/40 were delivered, with another 40 ordered during 1944, of which only 16 were completed before the war ended. This last batch became the K 39/41, again with provision for a muzzle brake, and with further manufacturing simplifications incorporated. These later models were among the few German guns able to fire the concrete-piercing Röchling projectiles.

All the variants in the K52 series were sound but heavy weapons that had to be installed on a firing platform. They were moved in up to four sections by mechanical means. The time into action was from six to eight hours, and once in action the rate of fire was at best three rounds in two minutes. Most were originally employed on the Eastern Front, although at least six fired into the Anzio bridgehead in Italy during late 1943. The demands of the Atlantic Wall meant that many were diverted to the coastal defence role. By March 1945 only eight examples of the K52 series were still deployed by batteries in the field.

Specification		
Calibre:	210mm	8.27in
Length of piece:	9,350mm	375.2in
Weight travelling (total):	59,100kg	130,290lb
Weight in action (approx):	39,800kg	87,743lb
Traverse:	360°	
Elevation:	-4 to +45°	
Muzzle velocity:	800m/s	2,625ft/sec
Max range:	34,000m	37,183yd
Shell weight:	135kg	297.7lb

Czechoslovakia
Skoda 240mm Model 16 Gun

The Skoda 240mm Model 16 gun was the partner to the 305mm Model 16 howitzer (qv), so it shared the same firing platform and carriage. Both were among the first generation of heavy artillery designed to be towed by special Daimler petrol-electric tractors in 'trains' consisting not only of the main gun loads but also of trailers for tools, ammunition, domestic arrangements and so on. A typical Model 16 gun train could consist of at least five main loads and 15 other vehicles, all so arranged that the great weights involved would be able to travel over rough terrain without too many problems. The Model 16 gun, a reinforced naval gun, was 40 calibres long and fired a 161kg (355lb) projectile to a range of 29,875m (32,672yd). The complete gun, once emplaced, weighed 86,000kg (189,595lb), so getting the gun in and out of action was slow and required a great deal of labour.

Nine guns were originally ordered but not all were finished by the end of 1918. Those completed saw some action on the Western Front and were then returned to Pilsen. Between the wars the type was adopted by the Czechoslovak army and they were updated with rubber-tyred wheels and generally kept serviceable. When the Germans took over in 1939 they took six guns into their own service (as the schwere 24cm Kanone (t)), still with their original Great War period tractors. They also ordered spare barrels and placed an order for an initial 6,100 updated projectiles, later increased to 12,500, although this total was never achieved.

The guns were fired during the Battle of France and for a while were installed near Calais to protect German shipping using the English Channel. In 1941, with the invasion of the Soviet Union, the guns were moved east (by railway) where at least two at any one time took part in the Siege of Leningrad. They continued to fire until the siege was lifted in early 1944. The two guns involved by then could not be moved before they were captured.

Throughout their service life a part of the Skoda works was kept busy preparing spare barrels (barrel life was 1,000 rounds) and generally repairing and refurbishing battle-worn guns and their carriages, while ammunition remained in production until 1945. By March 1945 only two guns remained available for service and they were destroyed by their crews during May that year. The one gun still remaining, under repair, was later scrapped.

Specification		
Calibre:	240mm	9.45in
Length of piece:	9,600mm	378in
Weight travelling (total):	143,000kg	315,255lb
Weight in action (approx):	86,000kg	189,595lb
Traverse:	360°	
Elevation, firing:	-5 to +41.5°	
Muzzle velocity:	794m/s	2,605ft/sec
Max range:	29,875m	32,672yd
Shell weight:	161kg	355lb

An emplaced Skoda 240mm Model 16 gun

Czechoslovakia
Skoda 149mm Model 14 Howitzer

By the end of the first decade of the 20th century, the Skoda Works at Pilsen had developed to the point where it had become one of the major armament works in Europe, second only to the mighty Krupp concern of Essen, Germany. Much of the Skoda output was for the Austro-Hungarian army (and navy) and among the many products designed and manufactured specifically for them was a 149.1mm (5.87in) howitzer of entirely conventional design and having a barrel 14 calibres long (L/14). It was introduced into Austro-Hungarian service during 1914 (hence the Model 14 designation), replacing a number of elderly in-service howitzers that still lacked recoil mechanisms. As with most

9

A Skoda 149mm Model 14 howitzer

Skoda products the Model 14 proved to be a sound, serviceable howitzer with a maximum range of 6,900m (7,550yd). The standard high-explosive projectile weighed a destructive 41kg (90.4lb).

Combat experience gained during the Great War proved the Model 14 to be so serviceable that the Czech, Austrian and Hungarian states that emerged after 1918 were happy to maintain the type in their respective armed services. Further Model 14s also went to Italy, either as captured war booty or as war reparations, becoming their Obice da 149/12. Many were still around in 1939, the Italian army alone having 490, and they continued to serve for some years. During the inter-war years, as and when funds allowed, some modifications were made to the Model 14 by all their various owners, mainly centred around alterations to make the original horse-drawn carriage amenable to mechanised traction. Most such attempts seem to have been limited to modifying the limber on which the trails were carried. Any increases in towing speed must have been slight, as the original spoked carriage wheels were retained, as were the travelling seats on the shield and limber for a few of the crew.

The Hungarian MAVAG concern did install rubber-tyred wheels onto at least some of the Hungarian army's Model 14s to make them the M.14/35. In 1938 the Model 14 entered German service following its take-overs of Austria and Czechoslovakia. It then became the 15cm sFH M.14 (Skoda) and was used by German heavy field artillery batteries, mainly in the Balkans. German stocks were increased after 1943 by any remaining Italian pieces that could be acquired. A few survivors managed to remain around until the end in 1945.

Specification		
Calibre:	149.1mm	5.87in
Length of piece:	2,090mm	71.11in
Weight travelling:	3,070kg	6,769lb
Weight in action:	2,344kg	5,168lb
Traverse:	5°	
Elevation:	-5 to +43°	
Muzzle velocity:	300m/s	984ft/sec
Max range:	6,900m	7,550yd
Shell weight:	41kg	90.4lb

Czechoslovakia
Skoda 149mm Model 14/16 Howitzer

The Skoda 149mm Model 14/16 howitzer may be considered an all-round improvement on the Model 14. Almost as soon as the Model 14 started to be used in action in 1914, it became apparent that the maximum angle of barrel elevation was too low for many fire missions carried out along the Austro-

Italian alpine borders, so a call went out for the necessary changes to be introduced. The howitzer's cradle was therefore redesigned to permit a maximum elevation of +70°. At the same time improvements were made to the propellant charge system to increase the maximum range, and further refinements were also made to the projectiles to make them slightly more streamlined – existing Model 14 projectiles could still be utilised. To accommodate the increased firing stresses the carriage and trail were strengthened. Slight alterations to the barrel resulted in it being marginally longer than that of the Model 14. The result, almost identical visibly to its predecessor, became the Skoda 149mm Model 14/16, replacing the Model 14 in production at Pilsen.

After 1914 the Model 14/16 became a standard weapon within the new Czechoslovak army, although by 1938 all had been withdrawn from service and stored, awaiting the scrap furnaces. Few were still around when the Germans marched in, so the Czechoslovak Model 14/16s never became part of the German artillery park.

The other post-1918 Model 14/16 recipient was Italy, where it became the Obice da 149/13, again as the result of war booty or reparations. The Italians thought highly of the Model 14/16, even though the rate of fire was limited to two rounds a minute, at best. They extended its utility during the late 1930s by introducing solid steel, rubber-tyred wheels for

mechanised traction by trucks, and changes to the gun shield contours. The Obice da 149/13 was employed extensively throughout all Italian campaigns conducted from 1940 to 1943, including those on the Eastern Front. Following Italy's surrender in September 1943, all available surviving examples were seized by the Germans and transferred for their own purposes, most being issued to German heavy field artillery batteries based in occupied Italy until the war ended. The German designation was 15cm sFH 401(i) and the following data relates to this version.

Specification		
Calibre:	149.1mm	5.87in
Length of piece:	2,120mm	83.45in
Weight travelling:	3,340kg	7,365lb
Weight in action:	2,765kg	6,097lb
Traverse:	6°	
Elevation:	-5 to +70°	
Muzzle velocity:	350m/s	1,148ft/sec
Max range:	8,970m	9,616yd
Shell weight:	40.33kg	88.9lb

Skoda 149mm Model 14/16 howitzer

Czechoslovakia
Skoda 149mm Model 25 Howitzer

The Skoda 149mm Model 25 howitzer was the first item of artillery designed by Skoda specifically for the new Czechoslovak government. It was originally intended that the new howitzer would replace the Skoda 149mm Model 14/16 but to simplify the logistic chain and utilise existing stocks of ammunition, the new howitzer had to fire the same ammunition family as the Model 14/16. Design work began during the early 1920s and the howitzer was approved for service during 1925; it

thus became the Model 25. Production for the Czechoslovak army (there were no export sales) continued at Pilsen until 1933, by which time the shortcomings of the Model 25 had become apparent.

The retention of the Model 14/16 ammunition family resulted in what was considered an inadequate range for a rather heavy piece, considering the calibre and the 18-calibre barrel. This weight factor was amplified by the Model 25 having to be transported in two sections for long moves. The enforced retention of horse traction in the place of expensive (for the then hardly established Czechoslovak state) mechanised towing units meant that the howitzer was too heavy to comfortably tow as one load. The carriage itself formed one load, with the barrel on a separate transport trailer. Laboriously getting the two sections apart and together again lengthened the time needed to get the Model 25 in and out of action, something that did not endear the howitzer to its crews. For short moves the Model 25 could be towed by a mechanised tractor as one load, but with care and at relatively low speeds, for the wooden-spoked wheels could not withstand severe jolting over rough terrain.

The acceptance of the Model 25's limitations meant that plans were formed for the Model 25 to be replaced by the mechanically towed Skoda 149mm Model 37 (K4) howitzer (qv). This programme had hardly begun when the Germans marched into Czechoslovakia in 1939, so many Model 25s remained in Czech service. The Model 25 then became part of the German gun park with the designation of 15cm sFH 25(t). During the early war years the Model 25 was a standard howitzer within the many German divisions that were completely equipped with impounded Czech matériel. Most 'German' Model 25s appear to have been withdrawn by 1942, only for 126 to be transferred to the Slovakian army allied to Germany.

Specification		
Calibre:	149.1mm	5.87in
Length of piece:	2,700mm	106.3in
Weight travelling:	6,050kg	13,338lb
Weight in action:	3,800kg	8,337lb
Traverse:	7°	
Elevation:	-5 to +72°	
Muzzle velocity:	450m/s	1,476ft/sec
Max range:	11,800m	12,910yd
Shell weight:	42kg	92.6lb

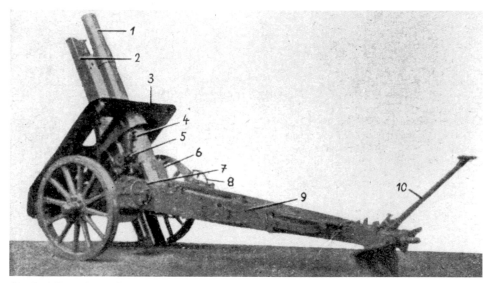

A textbook illustration of a Skoda 149mm Model 25 howitzer

Czechoslovakia
Skoda 149mm Model 33 (K1) Howitzer

By the early 1930s, Skoda designers were not only taking note of what artillery developments were in progress elsewhere, but were highly active in introducing design innovations of their own. They noted that almost everywhere the once-stubby howitzer barrels were growing in length to increase potential range while retaining the adjustable, separate bagged propellant charges inherent in all howitzers. Their carriages were also changing. Mechanised traction was fast becoming the norm for many armies, although the horse still remained the main means of towing artillery in many instances, mainly for economic reasons. It was also noted that split trails offered not only a high degree of barrel traverse,

Preparing to remove the barrel of a Romanian Skoda 149mm Model 33 (K1) howitzer – for transport

enabling gunners to switch rapidly from one target to another, but also greater firing stability in action.

Skoda accordingly incorporated these design features in their K series of howitzers, the first of which, the K1, was introduced in 1933. The Model 33 (K1) did have a split-trail carriage and steel, rubber-tyred wheels but it retained the ability to be towed by horse teams as well as mechanised tractors. For horse towing the barrel could be separated from the carriage in a less labour-intensive manner than before, and then towed on a special transporter. The relatively long 27-calibre barrel endowed the Model 33 (K1) with a significant maximum range improvement over what had been possible from previous 149mm howitzers, even though the ammunition remained based around the Model 14/16 family.

The Czechoslovak army tested the Model 33 (K1) and were sufficiently impressed to request further development, but none were ordered. Instead the Model 33 (K1) went into production as an export model, with sales made to Turkey, Yugoslavia and Romania. The numbers involved are not known but cannot have been many. The Romanian army fielded their Model 33 (K1) batteries alongside the German army on the Eastern Front in 1941 and 1942 but thereafter most appear to have been lost. The small batch delivered to Yugoslavia (probably not more than 18, intended to form a Corps artillery battalion) was taken over by the Germans in 1941. Although the type was allotted the designation of 15cm sFH 402(j) they do not appear to have been utilised by Germany other than for duties with garrison units based within Yugoslavia.

Specification		
Calibre:	149.1mm	5.87in
Length of piece:	4,050mm	159.5in
Weight travelling:	5,820kg	12,833lb
Weight in action:	5,020kg	11,069lb
Traverse:	45°	
Elevation:	-5 to +70°	
Muzzle velocity:	570m/s	1,870ft/sec
Max range:	15,100m	16,250yd
Shell weight:	42kg	92.6lb

A Skoda 149mm Model 33 (K1) howitzer as supplied to Yugoslavia

Czechoslovakia
Skoda 149mm Model 37 (K4) Howitzer

German gunners in action with a 15cm sFH 37(t), the Skoda 149mm Model 37 (K4) howitzer

As mentioned in the previous entry, Czechoslovak army ordnance specialists tested the 149mm Model 33 (K1) howitzer but decided a version developed to more closely meet their particular specifications was preferable. Armed with a new list of requirements, the Skoda designers set about making the Model 33 (K1) suitable for mechanised traction only, by then an army priority. Under the Skoda design designation of 'K4', this involved changes to the carriage, and especially to the rubber-tyred wheels, but the howitzer barrel was also altered. In order to ensure the developed howitzer was a better-balanced single load while being towed, the barrel was shortened slightly. Adjustments were made to the top propelling charges to increase the maximum muzzle velocity, thereby obtaining the same maximum range as the Model 33 (K1).

Numerous other minor modifications were introduced, the result being made ready for testing in 1936. It was accepted for service the following year and ordered into series production as the Model 37 (K4), along with its tractor unit, the fully tracked Praga T6. In numerous ways the Model 37 (K4) was well in advance of many of its contemporaries, combining high mobility, a useful maximum range and a general 'handiness' in place of the cumbersome, time-consuming handling procedures of the previous era. In addition the wide angle of traverse (45°), made possible by the split-trail carriage, enabled the gun crews to rapidly switch from one target to another without traversing the entire carriage, and even realistically track and engage direct-fire targets such as tanks.

The Model 37 (K4) was supposed to replace the 149mm Model 25 as soon as could be managed, although it took a while to establish the Model 37 (K4) line. The first examples were only just beginning to roll off the line when the Germans marched in and took over the Skoda production facilities at Pilsen. Only a few examples reached the Czechoslovak army for field trials. Noting the modernity and all-round performance of the Model 37 (K4), the Germans decided to retain the production line in being for their own purposes, so many Wehrmacht divisions were eventually issued with what they knew as the 15cm sFH 37(t). In time, examples were diverted to equip at least part of the Slovakian army heavy artillery park.

Specification		
Calibre:	149.1mm	5.87in
Length of piece:	3,600mm	142in
Weight travelling:	5,730kg	12,635lb
Weight in action:	5,200kg	11,466lb
Traverse:	45°	
Elevation:	-5 to +70°	
Muzzle velocity:	580m/s	1,903ft/sec
Max range:	15,100m	16,250yd
Shell weight:	42kg	92.6lb

Czechoslovakia
Skoda 210mm Model 18 and 18/19 Howitzers

Until the Great War years Skoda concentrated on two heavy howitzer calibres for the Austro-Hungarian army, 149.1mm (5.87in) and 305mm (12in). Even before 1914 it was felt that an interim calibre of 210mm (8.27in) would be useful, the result being the Skoda 210mm Model 16. This was a simple design that, due to being confined to towing by horse teams, had to be broken down into as many as five loads. The Model 16 was such a heavy weapon for its calibre that ordnance technicians considered it as delivering insufficient range to justify its retention.

A complete revision of the design was thus undertaken, resulting in the Model 18. The barrel was lengthened from 14 calibres to 16 and the projectile and propellant charge system was considerably revised to generate the better maximum range required. The Model 18 fired from a steel firing platform, carried as one load, with the cradle and barrel forming another two horse-drawn loads. A fourth load included all the devices, tools and other accessories needed to assemble and service the howitzer once at a carefully surveyed firing site. The Model 18 thus emerged as a ponderous weapon, but as it was intended for static warfare, such as the reduction of fortifications, it was considered acceptable and was retained by the newly formed Czechoslovak army after 1918.

The Model 18 was still around in 1939 (the Model 16 having been long-gone by then), but it had been joined by the Model 18/19. This model retained the ordnance and ammunition suite of the Model 18 but allied to a revised cradle intended from the outset to be towed by mechanical traction. The Model 18/19 cradle and barrel could then be carried combined and moved as a single load slung between two special rubber-tyred transporter axles.

During the inter-war years these howitzers were rarely fired, so by 1939, the year of the German take-over of Czechoslovakia, they were still available and serviceable. They therefore entered the German armoury as the 21cm Mrs 18(t) or 18/19(t) and issued to heavy artillery batteries commanded at Corps or army level. A total of 22 howitzers were involved (the Germans referred to the pieces as Mörser – Mrs), along with about 6,900 rounds. They were used in action, notably during the Siege of Leningrad. By 1945 there were only 17 left, along with just 183 rounds.

Specification		
Calibre:	210mm	8.27in
Length of piece:	3,360mm	132in
Weight travelling (total):	25,050kg	55,225lb
Weight in action (approx):	9,460kg	20,860lb
Traverse:	360°	
Elevation:	+40 to +71.5°	
Muzzle velocity:	380m/s	1,247ft/sec
Max range:	10,100m	11,050yd
Shell weight:	135kg	297.7lb

Preparing a Skoda 210mm Model 18/19 howitzer for action

Czechoslovakia
Skoda 220mm Model 28 (ONa) Howitzer

The Skoda 220mm Model 28 (ONa) was the howitzer equivalent of the 149mm Model 28 (NOa) gun, sharing the same cradle, firing platform and many design features. Developed as a private venture specifically for the export market as the Czechoslovak army had no need for such an equipment, the Model 28 (ONa) was designed from the beginning to be towed by mechanised tractors in three or four loads.

The main customer was Poland, where the Model 28 (ONa) was known as the 220mm mozdzierz wzor 32 (wzor – model), forming the only super-heavy artillery component of the Polish army. They purchased 27 examples, along with a locally developed full-tracked tractor based on a Vickers 6-ton tank chassis and known as the C7P, to tow them, all organised into a single artillery regiment from 1932 onwards. Great propaganda use was made of them by parades and displays to demonstrate Poland's intention to defend itself, something which went badly wrong in September 1939, due mainly to the speed of events, which did not allow the howitzers to make much display of their capabilities. As a result of the lightning-speed German invasion, almost all the Polish howitzers fell into German hands. At least 14 of them were captured intact and ready to be adopted, together with their tractors, into the German fold as the 22cm Mrs (p) – it seems the remainder were used for spare parts.

The other customer for the 220mm Model 28 (ONa) was Yugoslavia. The size of the batch for this

nation was probably not more than 12. All had been delivered well before the war reached the Balkans, but no record can be found of any subsequent use of them, either by the Yugoslavs or the Germans – the German army issued the reporting designation of 22cm Mrs 538(j).

For both customers the Model 28 (ONa) had a 19-calibre barrel providing a useful range of 14,200m (15,530yd). For long moves the barrel, weighing 7,300kg (16,094lb), was carried as a single load, although, for short moves, it was possible to carry the combined cradle and barrel slung between special transporter axles. The prefabricated steel firing platform was also towed as a single load. As the barrel had to be lowered from angles above +40° between each firing, the rate of fire was limited to, at best, one round a minute.

Specification		
Calibre:	220mm	8.66in
Length of piece:	4,340mm	170.8in
Weight travelling (total):	22,700kg	50,045lb
Weight in action:	14,700kg	32,405lb
Traverse:	360°	
Elevation, firing:	+40 to +75°	
Muzzle velocity:	500m/s	1,640ft/sec
Max range:	14,200m	15,530yd
Shell weight:	128kg	282.2lb

Polish Skoda 220mm Model 28 (ONa) howitzers on parade, towed by their C7P tractors

Czechoslovakia
Skoda 305mm Model 16 Howitzer

As mentioned earlier, the Skoda 305mm Model 16 howitzer was the partner to the 240mm Model 16 gun and shared the same prefabricated firing platform and carriage. However, being much lighter than the Model 16 gun it did not need the expensive petrol-electric tractors, relying instead on

more conventional tractors. In general terms it was an updated development of an earlier Skoda howitzer, the 305mm Model 11. The stubby barrel was only 12 calibres long, so it had a limited range. Owing mainly to the need to lower the barrel between firings and the weight and size of the

Textbook illustration of a Skoda 305mm Model 16 howitzer

almost vertically at almost all combat ranges.

After 1918 the Model 16 was taken over by the Czechoslovak army and modernised to be carried in only two loads, the barrel and carriage being moved complete, slung between two transporter axles. An undefined number (probably not more than six) were passed to Yugoslavia during the early 1920s. By 1939 there were still 17 examples in Czechoslovak service.

From 1939 onwards all these howitzers, including the Yugoslav examples, fell into German hands intact. Despite their bulk and weight they were deemed suitable for issue to Wehrmacht heavy batteries, where they were known as the 30.5cm Mrs (t). Their service appears to have been limited to what they were best for, namely siege warfare. They were fired against Leningrad, where at least six were always in the firing line, only to be captured when the siege was lifted in early 1944. More were deployed during the Siege of Sevastopol. That seems to have been the limit of their active service, as by March 1945 only 13 were still available for use, along with 5,643 projectiles still waiting to be fired. Apart from a few diverted to museums they were all scrapped soon after the war ended. There was also a Skoda 380mm (15in) Model 16 howitzer but none remained serviceable by 1939.

projectiles utilised, the rate of fire was never better than one round every five minutes.

The Model 16 was designed for travel through alpine regions, so by 1918 they were deployed along the Austro-Italian border and took part in the demolitions of Italian fortifications, their delayed-action fuzes having considerable effect. Both high-explosive and concrete-penetrating projectiles were available. Two propellant charge systems provided an extensive array of range overlaps at various barrel elevation angles, allowing projectiles to descend

Specification		
Calibre:	305mm	12in
Length of piece:	3,660mm	144in
Weight travelling (total):	38,500kg	84,876lb
Weight in action (approx):	23,150kg	51,036lb
Traverse:	360°	
Elevation, firing:	+40 to +75°	
Muzzle velocity:	448m/s	1,470ft/sec
Max range:	12,300m	13,450yd
Shell weight:	289kg	637lb

Czechoslovakia
Skoda 420mm Model 17 Howitzer

The Skoda 420mm Model 17 howitzer had its origins in a pre-1914 coastal defence weapon designed with the intention that one hit would destroy any Dreadnought class warship. One such weapon was installed in an armoured turret to defend the Austro-Hungarian naval base at Pola (now Pula) on the Adriatic: that was the Model 14. Skoda were also asked to develop a 420mm howitzer for land service, the first result being the Model 16. This model involved the same petrol-electric tractor train as the 240mm Model 16 gun and had to be moved in five main sections, plus the usual following of other vehicles. After a redesign the firing platform was reduced in size so the number of main loads was then reduced to four. This revised version became the

420mm Model 17. Only one Model 17 was anywhere ready by the time the war ended, so it did not see action, although at least seven examples of earlier Skoda 420mm howitzers did.

The Model 17 was a ponderous beast, the 15-calibre barrel assembly weighing 100,000kg (220,460lb) just by itself. Maximum range firing a 1,020kg (2,249lb) projectile was 14,600m (15,966yd), with a two-part propellant charge system ensuring that the projectile descended vertically onto its target at all lesser ranges. The solitary Model 17 remained in the workshops at Pilsen until 1940, displayed as an example of Skoda's technical expertise.

During 1940 the Germans decided that the 17

howitzer would be useful against the French Maginot Line, so it was refurbished, the maximum elevation angle was increased to +71.5° and a few other alterations were made. At that time ammunition stocks stood at 1,223 concrete-penetrating and high-explosive rounds. The howitzer was then emplaced near Saarbrücken and fired against Fort Schönenbourg during the Battle of France, but the results were indifferent against the well-protected main structures, the fort remaining still intact when an armistice was arranged.

After that the howitzer, by then known as the 42cm Mrs 17(t), was set aside until 1942. It was then laboriously moved, by rail, to the Crimea to play its part in the final attack on Sevastopol, firing a total of 192 rounds. After that the howitzer needed a new barrel liner, but it was never manufactured. Exactly what became of the sole 42cm Mrs 17(t) is uncertain, although it may survive somewhere in Russia.

Specification		
Calibre:	420mm	16.5in
Length of piece:	6,290mm	247in
Weight travelling (total):	160,000kg	352,734lb
Weight in action (approx):	105,000kg	231,480lb
Traverse:	360°	
Elevation, firing:	+40 to +71°	
Muzzle velocity:	435m/s	1,427ft/sec
Max range:	14,600m	15,966yd
Shell weight:	1,020kg	2,250lb

The sole Skoda 420mm Model 17 howitzer ready to fire

France
Canon de 145 L mle 1916 St Chamond

The opening of the Great War in 1914 found the French army seriously short of artillery, as they did not anticipate involvement in a long war involving trench warfare. By August 1915 the heavy-artillery duel between the French and German armies was becoming so dominated by the German batteries that desperate measures were considered. One was the employment of 138.6mm (5.456in) naval barrels placed on hastily designed land carriages. Two models of gun barrel were involved, one dating from 1891 and 45 calibres long. The other (and preferred) gun dated from 1910 and was 55 calibres long. As the stocks of 138.6mm ammunition were limited and unsuitable for land warfare, both types of barrel were bored to a new calibre of 145mm (5.7in) at the government arsenal at St Chamond. New 145mm ammunition was placed in production at the same time as the guns were being converted. Neither of the rebored 145mm gun conversions was considered satisfactory for the land role but they had to be retained because heavy artillery was in short supply. As soon as possible after 1918, surviving guns were withdrawn and stockpiled against some future need.

The mle 1916 was a somewhat cumbersome and unbalanced weapon but it could be moved as a single load, although at a very slow pace, by a heavy tractor. For this the trails were joined together on a limber with a single axle steered round sharp bends by a member of the crew seated above the limber.

Time in and out of action was at least three hours and the maximum rate of fire possible was eight rounds in five minutes.

The 145mm guns remained unemployed from 1918 until 1939, some barrels being passed to the French navy. In 1939 survivors were withdrawn from their gun sheds and once again prepared for battle. Plans were laid to replace surviving non-standard 145mm barrels with new 155mm (6.1in) components (see following entry) but this never happened. The plans were overtaken by the speed of events of May/June 1940, and the German army found itself the owner of some serviceable but decidedly non-standard long-range artillery. As early as 1942 the 145mm guns were being installed as part of the Atlantic Wall defences, along with all available ammunition. They were meant to be interim weapons until something better came along but most were still there in 1945.

Specification		
Calibre:	145mm	5.7in
Length of piece:	7,362mm	289.8in
Weight travelling:	14,060kg	31,002lb
Weight in action:	13,210kg	29,128lb
Traverse:	6°	
Elevation, firing:	0 to +38°	
Muzzle velocity:	784m/s	2,572ft/sec
Max range:	20,200m	22,100yd
Shell weight:	36.2kg	79.8lb

Canon de 145 L mle 1916 St Chamond

France
Canon de 155 L mle 1916 St Chamond

The improvised 145mm mle 1916 naval guns mentioned in the previous entry were deemed unsatisfactory on several counts, one of them being that their ammunition was non-standard and further complicated the already overstretched French artillery logistic chain. A simple solution was to hand, as the 145mm barrels could either be rebored further, to 155mm (6.1in) when worn, or new

Canon de 155 L mle 1916 St Chamond carrying out coastal defence duties for the Germans as the 15.5cm K 420(f)

155mm barrels could be manufactured. In the event both approaches were adopted from April 1917 onwards, pending the introduction of a purpose-built 155mm gun that eventually emerged as the 155mm-long mle 1917. This meant that the enlarged-calibre mle 1916 gun could utilise 155mm projectiles and propellant charges of several types, all of them in mass production and available.

The continuing demand for heavy artillery during 1917 and 1918 meant that both the 145mm and 155mm mle 1916 naval gun conversions had to be retained until the Great War ended. After 1918 the 155mm mle 1916 guns followed the same path to artillery storage depots as their 145mm counterparts and there they remained until 1939.

As soon as World War II started, plans were laid to recommence the manufacture of new 155mm barrels and carriages, and enlarge all surviving 145mm barrels to 155mm, to introduce a measure of standardisation between two equipments that differed in appearance only in calibre-related aspects. Even in 1939 this was intended to be carried out at a slow pace of six guns every month, but work had not even commenced at St Chamond when the Germans invaded.

In 1939 the mle 1916 guns were still towed by their original Latil wheeled tractors, which had been in storage since 1918. They therefore moved from position to position at a maximum speed of 8km/h (5mph), although only over good roads, and they still took at least three hours to prepare for action. In early 1940 the French army had mobilised 152 of both calibres of gun, the 155mm being the most numerous. After May/June 1940, during which period the mle 1916s could contribute little due to their relatively static nature, the German army took over any that remained and incorporated them into the Atlantic Wall defences, where their long range made them useful assets. Undefined numbers of 155mm mle 1916 guns were also passed to Italy after 1918. The Italians developed a heavier projectile (47kg/103.6lb) for their guns, but they appear to have been little used after 1940.

Specification		
Calibre:	155mm	6.1in
Length of piece:	7,362mm	289.8in
Weight travelling:	14,000kg	30,870lb
Weight in action:	13,150kg	28,996lb
Traverse:	6°	
Elevation, firing:	0 to +38°	
Muzzle velocity:	790m/s	2,592ft/sec
Max range:	21,300m	23,300yd
Shell weight:	43kg	94.8lb

France
Matériel de 155 L mle 1877/1914

The Matériel de 155 L mle 1877/1914 was a hasty 1914 combination of the elderly 155mm (6.1in) De Bange mle 1877 siege gun barrel, 27 calibres long, with a more modern carriage devised by the Schneider concern. The original mle 1877 carriage lacked any form of recoil mechanism, other than inclined ramps along which the recoiling gun and carriage could travel before the total mass overcame the rearward momentum. They therefore had a slow rate of fire, as the gun had to be resighted between each firing. The 1914 Schneider carriage, although rather high and awkward-looking, did have a recoil mechanism, so it could fire more frequently (three rounds a minute) and, if required, it could be towed by mechanical tractors as well as horse teams. (Despite the 1914 conversions there were still numbers of the original mle 1877 in the French army inventory in 1939). The new combination became the Matériel de 155 L mle 1877/1914 Schneider and continued to fire the family of ammunition originally designed for the 1877 De Bange model.

During the Great War the Matériel de 155 L mle 1877/1914 was employed mainly in the counter-battery role and proved to be an adequate heavy gun when it was needed most, especially after modernised ammunition was introduced to increase the maximum range slightly. For horse traction the gun could be broken down into two sections, the barrel being towed on a pair of transporter axles and the carriage (and shield) on its own wheels. For short distances the complete gun could be towed by a mechanical tractor, but long moves still involved two loads and a maximum speed over good roads of 12km/h (7.5mph).

After 1918, remaining mle 1877/1914 guns were mainly relegated to fortress duties or were passed to

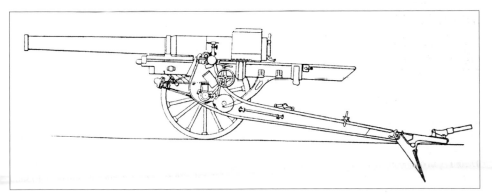

Cross-section drawing of the Matériel de 155 L mle 1877/1914

The barrel section of a horse-drawn Matériel de 155 L mle 1877/1914

reserve batteries. Some of them were provided with wider rubber-tyred wheels to assist mechanised traction. In 1940 there were still 83 serviceable examples 'on the books', only for them to pass into German hands after May/June 1940. It seems their booty was scrapped or issued only to garrison formations based in France. One offshoot from between the wars was that at some stage a small batch of these guns was somehow passed to the Soviet Union. What became of them has not been found recorded.

Specification		
Calibre:	155mm	6.1in
Length of piece:	4,200mm	165.4in
Weight travelling:	6,353kg	14,005lb
Weight in action:	6,010kg	13,252lb
Traverse:	4.6°	
Elevation, firing:	+5 to +40°	
Muzzle velocity:	561m/s	1,840ft/sec
Max range:	13,600m	14,873yd
Shell weight:	42.9kg	94.6lb

France
Matériel de 155 L mle 1917

By 1917 the imbalance between the French and German heavy artillery arms was becoming most pronounced in favour of the Germans. Not only was the French artillery arm frequently outnumbered but they were increasingly being outranged. French staff officers called for a new 155mm (6.1in) gun with a range of at least 16,000m (17,500yd) but to fully develop such a gun and a suitable carriage would absorb valuable time and resources. It was once again time for another hasty improvisation to at least partially rectify the situation. This time the Schneider carriage devised for the Matériel de 155 L mle 1877/1914 was much modified to carry a new and longer barrel designed by Schneider. Once

completed and tested the resultant Matériel de 155 L mle 1917 was rushed into service. Replacements of the shorter-barrelled piece were carried out by the hundred at the Schneider Le Creusot factory. It also seems that new barrel and carriage combinations were manufactured.

The mle 1917 barrel was approximately 32 calibres long, capable of firing a standard 155mm high-explosive projectile weighing 43.1kg (95lb) to a highly respectable 17,300m (18,925yd) – more than specified. A counterbalance weight was added over the breech to alleviate the inevitable muzzle preponderance imposed by the weight of the longer barrel. The mle 1914 carriage was considerably

A captured Matériel de 155 L mle 1917 in a coastal emplacement as the German-designated 15.5cm K 416(f)

modified to allow the long barrel and carriage combination to be towed by mechanised traction in one piece. For this the barrel was drawn back and clamped over the box trail to present a more balanced load. For horse traction two ten-horse teams were necessary, the barrel being towed on a twin-axle transporter. By 1918, 420 mle 1917 guns had been issued, with more being finished later to complete contracts.

In 1940 the quantity of guns in French artillery depots was 535, despite an unknown number, probably not more than 12, having been passed to Belgium during the inter-war years (one still survives in the Brussels War Museum). After mid-1940 the German army was happy to press as many survivors as could be recovered for the usual fate of incorporation into the Atlantic Wall defences, a role for which the gun's useful maximum range made it entirely suitable. The Matériel de 155 L mle 1917 then became the 15.5cm K 416(f).

Specification		
Calibre:	155mm	6.1in
Length of piece:	4,680mm	184.25in
Weight travelling: one load	9,900kg	21,830lb
Weight in action:	8,956kg	19,748lb
Traverse:	4.5°	
Elevation, firing:	-5 to +40°	
Muzzle velocity:	665m/s	2,182ft/sec
Max range:	17,300m	18,925yd
Shell weight:	43.1kg	95lb

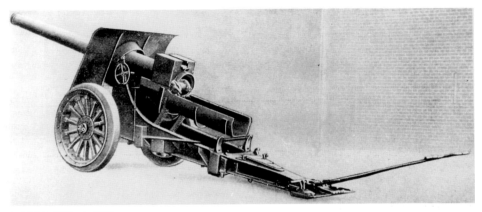

Matériel de 155 L mle 1917

France
Matériel de 155 mle 1918

During the Great War French army ordnance authorities had to sanction several hasty conversions and barrel and carriage combinations. One of them was accepted as late as 1918, for by then the demands from the Western Front for heavy artillery were still pouring in. Although excellent pieces, such as the 155mm GPF (qv) were coming off the production lines, they were doing so at a time when priorities were being directed to providing the newly arriving American forces with war matériel of all kinds, including artillery. As a stopgap, Schneider proposed placing still-available 155mm (6.1in) mle 1877 De Bange gun barrels, as already used once for the Matériel de 155 L mle 1877/1914 (qv) but still recognised as a useful gun, onto yet another type of carriage. This time the carriage was that of the Schneider 155mm C 17 S howitzer (qv), readily available due to the large numbers then in production. Despite the urgency of the situation at that time it seems that not only were existing mle

1877 barrels utilised for the conversion, but new barrels were manufactured as well.

Whatever the case, the old barrel design was updated to enable it to fire more modern ammunition and deliver more range. Both high-explosive and armour-penetrating projectiles were involved. To balance the barrel preponderance on the carriage an extra counterweight was added over the breech. The box-trail howitzer carriage was employed without its usual shield and it proved possible to tow the entire gun and carriage as a single load, either by a mechanical tractor or a team of ten horses. Time in and out of action at a field site was 20 minutes, although if a firing platform was required the time was increased to three hours.

Production of the Matériel de 155 mle 1918 by Schneider continued even after 1918 to complete contracts, but it seems that the gun-and-carriage combination was little used between the wars, but was maintained in case of some future requirement. 23

The bulk of the Matériel de 155 mle 1918

In 1940 there were still 120 guns in French army artillery depots, many still in an as-new condition. Although most of them were prepared for service, all destined for motorised traction, few of them seem to have participated in the Battle of France. The Wehrmacht used whatever they could recover for incorporation into the Atlantic Wall defences as the 15.5cm K 425(f).

Specification		
Calibre:	155mm	6.1in
Length of piece:	4,089mm	161in
Weight travelling:	5,530kg	12,194lb
Weight in action:	5,050kg	11,135lb
Traverse:	6°	
Elevation, firing:	+1.25 to +43.5°	
Muzzle velocity:	561m/s	1,840ft/sec
Max range:	13,600m	14,873yd
Shell weight:	43.1kg	95lb

France
Matériel de 155 GPF

Commandant Fillioux, of the French artillery, had his own ideas regarding future artillery requirements. Before 1914 he had been involved in several artillery improvement projects. His ideas for a long-range 155mm (6.1in) gun presented before 1914 were overlooked as there seemed to be no requirement for such a weapon – the 75mm mle 1897 field gun seemed to be all that was necessary. By 1916 that had all changed, so Fillioux could once again present his project. This time it was accepted, as the French army had requested a gun with a range of at least 16,000m (17,500yd), provision for high-speed towing, and a wide angle of traverse to enable one gun to cover a wide target area.

The result was the prototype that nearly all other future artillery pieces were to follow, the Matériel de 155 GPF (the GPF denoted 'Grand Puissance Fillioux'). For the GPF a long, slender 38-calibre barrel was placed on a split-trail carriage with a suspension capable of being towed across rough terrain. By drawing the barrel back over the joined trails on a limber, the GPF formed a well-balanced single load. In the firing position the split-trail carriage formed a steady firing platform with a wide angle of traverse (60°). Overall the GPF was one of the best artillery designs of its day and for long after, its range of 19,500m (21,330yd) far exceeding the original 1916 requirement. The GPF went into series

A Matériel de 155 GPF recaptured by the Allies from the Afrika Korps in North Africa

production during 1917, at last giving the French artillery a chance to counter their enemies on a realistic scale.

When American troops arrived in France they at once recognised the value of the GPF and placed substantial orders to equip their own forces. The orders were so substantial that deliveries to the French army were affected, leading to the stopgap Matériel de 155 mle 1918 (see previous entry). After 1918 the US army adopted the GPF as the M1917 and M1918 (qv). By 1939 the GPF was still one of the most 'modern' artillery pieces the French army owned – they had 352 in 1940. Most of the French holdings were taken over intact by the Wehrmacht, who in turn adopted the GPF as one of their standard field pieces, as the 15.5cm K 418(f). These guns were also incorporated into the Atlantic Wall in significant numbers.

Specification		
Calibre:	155mm	6.1in
Length of piece:	5,725mm	225.4in
Weight travelling:	11,703kg	25,800lb
Weight in action:	10,750kg	23,407lb
Traverse:	60°	
Elevation, firing:	0 to +35°	
Muzzle velocity:	735m/s	2,411ft/sec
Max range:	19,500m	21,330yd
Shell weight:	43kg	94.8lb

A German recognition-manual illustration of a Matériel de 155 GPF

France
Matériel de 155 GPF-T

After 1918 the 155mm GPF (see previous entry) became the subject of trials and projects intended to improve the product and increase performance. One of them, the 155 GPF-CA, was an odd variant with revised chamber dimensions that entailed special ammunition. The purpose of this project is still uncertain, for it decreased the maximum range to 16,500m (18,050yd), with the result that few were manufactured, and none survived in 1939.

Far more successful was an overall modification of the GPF to improve travelling speeds. This updating project was overseen by one Capitaine Touzzard, who replaced the original pair of GPF wheels with two pneumatic tyres each side, both on a shock-absorbing suspension that increased the maximum towing speed from a steady 8km/h (5mph) to 25km/h (15.5mph). At the same time the limber assembly wheels were also converted to pneumatic. The opportunity was also taken to utilise inter-war ballistic developments involving the ammunition and propellant charges to increase the range to 21,000m (22,965yd). As the original 38-calibre barrel was retained, this increase was achieved mainly by lengthening the chamber to accommodate larger propellant charges, and lengthening the elevation arc to provide a maximum elevation of +39°. The result of all these changes was the Matériel de 155 GPF-T, with the T denoting 'Touzzard'. It was the most modern of all the French artillery pieces in service in 1940, carrying the GPF concept one stage further and in the process laying the foundations for future artillery developments that survive to this day.

Funding difficulties prevented the GPF-T update programme starting until 1939, so by the time the Germans invaded in May 1940 the French army had only 24, with another 24 either awaiting delivery or nearly completed. All of them fell into German hands virtually undamaged. The Germans were delighted with this haul, for they thought very highly of the GPF-T, taking the type into service as one of their standard field pieces, the 15.5cm K 419(f). Batteries supporting the Afrika Korps were provided with this gun. Not all the 15.5cm K 419(f) guns were sent to North Africa, for many were installed all along the Atlantic Wall, usually on turntables on circular concrete platforms to provide a wide arc of fire. The GPF carriage was also considered for the 12.8cm PaK 81/1 heavy anti-tank gun of 1944/1945.

Specification		
Calibre:	155mm	6.1in
Length of piece:	5,725mm	225.4in
Weight travelling:	13,700kg	30,423lb
Weight in action:	12,200kg	26,900lb
Traverse:	60°	
Elevation, firing:	0 to +39°	
Muzzle velocity:	735m/s	2,411ft/sec
Max range:	21,000m	22,965yd
Shell weight:	43kg	94.8lb

Two examples of the Matériel de 155 GPF-T in a North African setting

A Matériel de 155 GPF-T recaptured by the Allies from the Afrika Korps in North Africa

France
Canon de 194mm GPF

Once the 155mm GPF was in service it was soon appreciated that the ordnance and ballistics involved could be modified for larger calibres. One possibility was soon achieved at the St Chamond establishment by boring out a 155mm (6.1in) barrel to a naval calibre, 164.6mm (6.8in). It was then discovered that a better all-round performance could be obtained from scaling up the GPF barrel design to 194mm (7.64in). The problem then arose that moving a barrel much heavier than that of the 155 GPF on a conventional carriage would create mobility problems. That difficulty was overcome by making the entire equipment self-propelled, the resultant Canon de 194mm GPF being one of the

Matériel de 155 GPF on show at the Aberdeen Proving Ground, Maryland, USA

very first self-propelled artillery systems. There was also a corresponding 280mm (11in) howitzer (qv).

Not surprisingly for a first attempt, the 194mm equipment was cumbersome and possessed only a mediocre measure of mobility. The equipment was arranged in two halves. One, the main tractor unit, carried 60 rounds and propelling charges, a petrol engine and an electrical generator. The engine drove the generator to produce electricity used to power electrical motors and drive the tracks. The second unit was a trailer carrying the gun barrel and all the loading and fire control arrangements as well as its own petrol-electric system, although the latter was normally used only when the unit was manoeuvring into a firing position. Electrical power could be transmitted from the generator vehicle to the trailer via a cable in an emergency.

Once in service this heavy combination proved to be slow, the maximum speed being, at best, 8km/h (5mph) and the complex mechanisms caused endless troubles, most of the drive chain being too flimsy for the loads imposed. Yet it was a start and the French army proposed that some 500 should be ordered.

The Armistice intervened and so production was terminated. By 1939 there were 49 still in existence. Of these just 26 were mobilised to meet the German onslaught of May 1940, when most 194mm GPFs were captured or destroyed. This equipment was one that the Germans did not take into their own service, although they did undertake trials with the ammunition carrier unit as a possible munitions carrier for other artillery equipments. Nothing came of the project. Many 194mm projectiles were later incorporated into beach defences as rudimentary anti-landing-craft mines.

Specification		
Calibre:	194mm	7.64in
Length of piece:	5,085mm	200.2in
Weight travelling:	56,100kg	123,677lb
Weight in action:	29,600kg	65,255lb
Traverse:	360°	
Elevation, firing:	0 to +36°	
Muzzle velocity:	725m/s	2,378ft/sec
Max range:	20,800m	22,747yd
Shell weight:	91.8kg	202.4lb

Loading a Matériel de 155 GPF onto a railway wagon

France
Matériel de 220 L mle 1917

By 1916 the long-range German heavy artillery was able to outrange its French equivalents, leading to urgent calls for countermeasures. One of the responses was yet another hasty improvisation

that was to prove highly effective but heavy to an extreme. This was the Matériel de 220 L mle 1917 from Schneider et Cie of Le Creusot, consisting of a long 35-calibre barrel on a simple but heavy box-

This illustration clearly shows the bulk of the Matériel de 220 L mle 1917

area. The 220 L mle 1917 was one of the guns that kept the German army at bay during the post-Verdun period when much of the front-line French army was in a state of mutiny.

The type was retained in French army service after 1918, and in 1940 there were 56 still 'on the books', with another 12 held in reserve. Thanks mainly to their lack of mobility, almost all these guns fell into German hands intact, along with about 21,700 rounds of ammunition, and they became the 22cm K 532(f). They were ideal candidates for the coastal artillery role so, set on turntables in circular gun emplacements, they were all assigned to the Atlantic Wall, including locations in the Channel Islands, along with all serviceable ammunition. As usual, they were regarded as interim guns until something better became available, but it never did. Many were still around in 1945.

girder carriage that had to be lowered onto a prepared platform before firing. The weight of the 220 L mle 1917 was such that powerful mechanical tractors were all that could move it, usually in two loads weighing 30,120kg (66,402lb) combined. The barrel alone weighed 13,520kg (29.806lb). The gun could be moved as a single load, but for extremely short distances only. Once at a pre-levelled firing site the gun required at least six hours and a great deal of manual labour to prepare for action, and just as long to get ready for a move, so the tactical mobility of the 220 L mle 1917 was practically nil.

Under Great War conditions these shortcomings could be tolerated, especially as the gun fired a 104.75kg (230.9lb) high-explosive projectile to a maximum range of 22,800m (24,934yd), at a steady rate of eight rounds every 15 minutes, even if it did take four soldiers to lift the projectile to the breech

Specification		
Calibre:	220mm	8.66in
Length of piece:	7,627.5mm	302in
Weight travelling:	30,120kg	66,402lb
Weight in action:	25,880kg	57,055lb
Traverse:	20°	
Elevation, firing:	0 to +37°	
Muzzle velocity:	766m/s	2,513ft/sec
Max range:	22,800m	24,934yd
Shell weight:	104.75kg	230.9lb

Heavy work – manhandling a Matériel de 220 L mle 1917 into position

Part way through assembling a Matériel de 240 à tracteur mle 1884 et 1917

The Matériel de 240 à tracteur mle 1884 heavy gun was originally a coastal defence variant of a naval gun. Both had been replaced before 1914 and the barrels stored away, only to be dragged out again when the French army's heavy-artillery crisis arose in 1916. The response of the St Chamond arsenal was to refurbish these guns, and their carriages, for the field role, the end result being the Matériel de 240 à tracteur mle 1884. As the starting point was a static coastal defence gun and mounting, it was not too surprising that the result for the gunners in the field was a massive piece of artillery, even larger and heavier then the cumbersome Schneider equivalent, the 220 L mle 1917 (see previous entry).

Open day for a battery of Matériel de 240 à tracteur mle 1884 et 1917

Due to its static carriage the gun had to be broken down into two main loads, each pulled by two tractors, with other vehicles carrying accessories, tools and ammunition. Although these loads could be towed by tractors, the usual practice was to make long moves on special railway trucks, the sections then being transferred to their road transporters and moved at slow speed (5km/h or 3.1mph) to a pre-prepared firing site. It then took at least 24 hours of hard work to prepare the gun for action. The gun had a maximum range of 18,000m (19,685yd), firing a powerful 161kg (355lb) projectile, so it proved ideal for its intended counter-battery role, even if its tactical mobility was negligible. As many of the mle 1884 barrels were already worn when they were prepared for service, new mle 1917 barrels were manufactured by St Chamond as replacements. The mle 1917 barrel was slightly longer than the mle 1887 original and employed a different rifling system, but the external ballistic characteristics were the same, so the range was not altered.

After 1918 these guns were retained against some possible future use, so in 1939 there were still 31 in the depots. Of these just 12 were selected for immediate service, only to pass into German hands after June 1940. Not surprisingly, the Wehrmacht had no use for such cumbersome antiques, so they inevitably ended up as part of the Atlantic Wall defences, the mle 1887 equipments reverting to their original role. Equipments with the mle 1887 barrel became the 24cm K 556(f), those with the mle 1917 barrel becoming the 24cm K 556/1(f).

Specification		
Calibre:	240mm	9.45in
Length of piece: (mle 1887)	6,700mm	263.8in
Weight travelling:	40,960kg	90,300lb
Weight in action:	31,000kg	68,342lb
Traverse:	10°	
Elevation, firing:	0 to +38°	
Muzzle velocity:	640m/s	2,100ft/sec
Max range:	18,000m	19,685yd
Shell weight:	161kg	355lb

France
Canon de 155 C mle 1917 Schneider

Canon de 155 C mle 1917 Schneider ready for loading

Until 1914 the French army saw no need for a 155mm (6.1in) howitzer, so when the Great War started they had none, apart from a few fortress models from the 1880s, all without recoil mechanisms. By 1915 the St Chamond arsenal had hurriedly devised a 155mm howitzer, 390 of which were manufactured before production priority switched to a better design. This was a Schneider commercial model based on a 152mm (6in) howitzer produced post-1905 for the Russian army. By 1916 the need for a 155mm field howitzer, imposed by trench warfare conditions, was such that the 'Russian' Schneider was adopted. It required only a change of calibre to 155mm to produce the Canon de 155 C mle 1917 Schneider, or C 17 S, which then went on to become one of the most produced and prolific of all French artillery products. With a 15.3-calibre barrel, it proved to be a sturdy and serviceable howitzer that was soon coming off the Le Creusot production lines by the hundred, with demand boosted by its adoption by the US army during 1918 (see 155mm Gun M1917A1 and M1918A1).

After 1918 large numbers of the C 17 S were either sold or handed out to numerous nations, including Belgium, Brazil, Finland, Greece, Italy, Yugoslavia, Poland and Romania. Although the Poles, Belgians and French lost their entire stocks to the Germans during 1939 and 1940, the C 17 S remained in the field with many other armies until 1945 and even after. In May 1940 the French army had 1,827 examples in the field, with a further 216 held in reserve, nearly all of them converted from horse to mechanised traction by the provision of wider, rubber-tyred wheels and suitable axle bearings. Tractors included light Citroen half-tracks.

Most of the French and other captured holdings were taken over by the Germans for several purposes. One was the inevitable incorporation into the Atlantic Wall (including some on special turntable mountings) while others were handed to

nations allied with Germany (such as Bulgaria) or retained for batteries assigned to German occupation forces. So much 155mm ammunition was captured in 1939–40 that the German army was still drawing on captured stockpiles until 1945. One of the projectiles developed for the C 17 S howitzer was the forerunner of the NATO standard 155mm HE M107, still in service with many armies to this day.

Specification		
Calibre:	155mm	6.1in
Length of piece:	2,332mm	91.8in
Weight travelling:	3,720kg	8,203lb
Weight in action:	3,300kg	7,275lb
Traverse:	6°	
Elevation, firing:	0 to +42.3°	
Muzzle velocity:	450m/s	1,476ft/sec
Max range:	11,300m	12,362yd
Shell weight:	43.61kg	96.16lb

The Finnish army on parade with the Canon de 155 C mle 1917 Schneider

France
Canon de 155 C mle 15 St Chamond

By late 1914 the French army at last acknowledged that the type of war they were involved in was one of static trench warfare and they needed heavier artillery than the famous 75mm (2.95in) mle 1897 field gun. An urgent requirement was raised for a 155mm (6.1in) howitzer, and both

Schneider and the government arsenal at St Chamond responded. The St Chamond response was a sturdy, unremarkable and rather uninspired design but it was to prove more than adequate. There was little time for thorough development, so the St Chamond howitzer, the Canon de 155 C mle 15

St Chamond, was rushed into production during 1915 and thereafter churned out by the hundred.

At 17.8 calibres, the barrel was rather long for a howitzer of the period, but it did provide a maximum possible range of 10,600m (11,596yd). However, in order to prevent excessive barrel erosion, this was usually limited to 9,800m (10,717yd). An unusual feature for the period was that it could be towed by horse teams as one load. Once in the field the mle 15 served alongside the Schneider C 17 S (qv), the two howitzers being regarded as of equal combat value, even though the mle 15 could deliver less range than the C 17 S.

After 1918 the mle 15 suffered the usual fate of most French Great War artillery by being retained in gun sheds with little activity other than routine maintenance. A few were sold off to various South American states.

That changed in 1939, when the French army mobilised once again and it was discovered that, together with the C 17 S, there were 1,827 howitzers ready to be fielded. That total was achieved even after a batch of 24 mle 15s had been sent to Finland as a gesture of solidarity during late 1939. Once in

Finland the mle 15 howitzers took part in the 1939–40 Winter War against the Soviet Union, all surviving to remain in Finnish army service until the early 1960s. In France the events of mid-1940 meant that the mle 15 fell into German hands and became the 15.5cm sFH 415(f). The Germans retained 198 of them and sufficient ammunition to last for years. Apart from being issued to German army garrison units based within France, the captured howitzers also saw action on the Eastern Front, while 12 were emplaced as coastal defence weapons along sectors of the Baltic coastline. Few survived after 1945.

Specification		
Calibre:	155mm	6.1in
Length of piece:	2,764mm	108.8in
Weight travelling:	3,680kg	8,511lb
Weight in action:	3,040kg	6,703lb
Traverse:	5.8°	
Elevation, firing:	-5 to +40°	
Muzzle velocity:	467m/s	1,204ft/sec
Max range:	10,600m	11,596yd
Shell weight:	43.5kg	95.9lb

The Canon de 155 C mle 15 St Chamond

France
Matériel de 220 C mle 1916 Schneider

The Matériel de 220 C mle 1916 Schneider was another heavy howitzer that entered the French army gun park via a commercial order for a 220mm (8.66in) howitzer placed by Russia prior to 1914. When it was realised during 1915 that the French army was seriously short of heavy artillery, the need could be at least partially fulfilled by adopting the 'Russian' model virtually unchanged so that the usual development phase could be considerably shortened. The first examples were in service during 1916 and were able to make use of existing stocks of 220mm De Bange siege howitzer ammunition dating from 1877.

The 220 C mle 1916 was basically a scaled-up version of what would become the 155mm C 17 S. It had a stubby 10.3-calibre barrel hurling a 100.5kg (221.5lb) high-explosive or concrete-penetrating projectile to a maximum range of 11,000m (12,030yd), although some references mention 10,860m (11,876yd). Loading was assisted by a loading tray travelling along rails located over the box trail, resulting in a rate of fire of six rounds in five minutes – quite rapid for a piece of its calibre. For moves the barrel was usually withdrawn from the carriage to be transported as a separate load on a special transport trailer – the carriage travelled on its wheels. For very short distances the complete howitzer could be towed as one load, but only with extreme care and at slow speeds (up to 5km/h, or 3.1mph). Tractors were employed for towing, the loads involved being regarded as too heavy and cumbersome for horse teams.

The 220 C mle 1916 proved to be accurate, producing plunging fire that was highly effective against field fortifications. The type was therefore produced in some numbers. The French army still had 462 examples in stock in September 1939, of which 376 had been rendered fit for field service by May 1940. Between the wars an undiscovered number had been passed to Belgium. Nearly all the survivors were taken over by the Wehrmacht after June 1940, most of them eventually travelling to the Eastern Front, where they are known to have been used during the Siege of Leningrad. What became of them after then is not known. The German designation was 22cm Mörser 531(f).

Specification		
Calibre:	220mm	8.66in
Length of piece:	2,278mm	89.7in
Weight travelling:	10,810kg	22,443lb
Weight in action:	5,800kg	12,787lb
Traverse:	6°	
Elevation, firing:	+10 to +65°	
Muzzle velocity:	415m/s	1,361ft/sec
Max range:	11,000m	12,030yd
Shell weight:	100.5kg	221.5lb

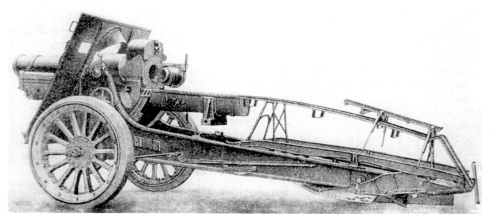

The Matériel de 220 C mle 1916 Schneider

The Matériel de 280 mle 1914 Schneider was another heavy howitzer that emerged as the result of Schneider private venture development for the Russian government. It was meant from the outset for the reduction of fixed fortifications and was adopted as such by the French army during 1914, although it was 1916 before the first production examples appeared. As might be expected from its intended role, the Matériel de 280 mle 1914 emerged as a large and heavy weapon with only a very limited degree of mobility as it was mounted on a platform set on the ground. To move the howitzer involved four main loads, one of which included the shield (a most unusual feature on such a heavy howitzer, although it was probably meant to protect the howitzer mechanisms, rather than the crew, from splinter damage). Two loads could be towed by a heavy-duty tractor. The barrel section alone weighed 6,150kg (13,558lb).

Once at a carefully surveyed and prepared firing site it took at least 16 hours and heavy work to prepare the howitzer for action and just as long to move out. During firings, the heavy 205kg (452lb) concrete-penetrating projectiles were delivered to the howitzer on carts and then lifted to the loading position by a small crane. As the barrel had to be

The Matériel de 280 mle 1914 Schneider

lowered from the firing elevation to a lower loading angle, the maximum possible rate of fire over prolonged periods was about 16 rounds an hour. The maximum range was 10,950m (11,975yd).

During the course of the Great War Schneider produced well over 100 examples of the 280 mle 1914 heavy howitzer, although between the wars the numbers dwindled slightly until there were about 100 left in their depots. They had no part to play during the Battle of France, thanks to their immobility, but the Wehrmacht immediately earmarked them for future use, bestowing the designation of 28cm Mörser 601(f) and training intensely with them. That use came during the Siege of Leningrad, when at least two of these howitzers were always ready for action from 1942 to 1944,

while another 21 (at least) served elsewhere on the Eastern Front. Eight of them participated in the attack on Sevastopol during 1942. Nearly all these Eastern Front examples had, by 1945, been either destroyed or captured by the Red Army.

Specification		
Calibre:	279.4mm	11in
Length of piece:	3,352mm	132in
Weight travelling:	24,820kg	54,718lb
Weight in action:	16,220kg	35,758lb
Traverse:	44.6°	
Elevation, firing:	+10 to +60°	
Muzzle velocity:	418m/s	1,371ft/sec
Max range:	10,950m	11,975yd
Shell weight:	205kg	452lb

France
Matériel de 280 mle 1914 sur chenilles

The Matériel de 280 mle 1914 Schneider was regarded so highly by the French army that they considered it for operations on the Western Front. During static trench warfare conditions it proved eminently suitable for such employment, but fluid warfare was expected to commence at some stage and the immobile heavy howitzer would therefore find limited applications. The solution was to place the howitzer on a self-propelled carriage, the same as that used for the Canon de 194mm GPF (qv). The Matériel de 280 mle 1914 sur chenilles (chenilles – caterpillar tracks) therefore travelled in two sections, the foremost carrying 40 rounds of ready-use

ammunition and the main petrol-electric power pack. The second section carried the howitzer, the same ordnance as for the Matériel de 280 mle 1914 Schneider. Originally the system was meant to carry a suitably modified 220mm (8.66in) C mle 1917. However, a single example remained the only prototype, a decision having been made to employ the heavier and more destructive 280 mle 1914 instead.

Since the howitzer and mobile platform combination was much heavier than for the 194mm model, the Matériel de 280 mle 1914 sur chenilles proved to be even more limited in mobility. Maximum speed was limited to 8km/h (5mph) and

The Matériel de 280 mle 1914 sur chenilles

the radius of action was only 25km (15.5 miles) over good going, and considerably less over rough terrain. As before, once at a firing position the two sections parted company, the howitzer section moving under its own petrol-electric power. As with the Canon de 194mm GPF, once in position the entire howitzer and platform could use its tracks for a full 360° traverse.

Although the St Chamond establishment manufactured nearly 30 of these equipments before the Armistice intervened, they appear to have been little used in action, the more fluid warfare of from August to September 1918 apparently leaving them floundering well to the rear. At that time arrangements were being made to mount the US 240mm (9.45in) M1918 howitzer (qv) in place of the 280mm howitzer, but it never happened. After 1918

a few were kept serviceable for display purposes and in May 1940 there were still 26 left. Once again they were little used, if at all, and the conquering Germans had no use for them. They all appear to have been scrapped.

Specification		
Calibre:	279.4mm	11in
Length of piece:	3,352mm	132in
Weight travelling:	55,000kg	121,252lb
Weight in action:	29,000kg	63,933lb
Traverse:	360°	
Elevation, firing:	0 to +60°	
Muzzle velocity:	418m/s	1,371ft/sec
Max range:	10,950m	11,975yd
Shell weight:	205kg	452lb

Germany
12.8cm Kanone 44

By 1943 the German army was being confronted by two unwelcome facts: their artillery was constantly outgunned, both in range and quantity, and the Soviet tank forces were growing in number and armoured protection. To make a quantum leap in countering this situation and after considering an interim Krupp design, the 12.8cm K 43, it was decided to go one stage

further and select a dual-purpose field and anti-tank gun, the 12.8cm K 44. Both Krupp and Rheinmetall-Borsig were given contracts to develop prototypes for trials, from which the Krupp submission emerged successful, due partially, at least, to the more complex six-wheeled carriage from Rheinmetall-Borsig.

The Krupp 12.8cm K 44 was a scaled-up version

The Rheinmetall-Borsig version of the 12.8cm K 44

of the 8.8cm PaK 43 anti-tank gun, then already in production, so it had a cruciform firing platform carried on four wheels and providing a full 360° traverse. The ordnance was a variant of the 12.8cm Flak 40 anti-aircraft gun and fired much the same ammunition, but with the addition of an anti-armour round. The ordnance on the K 44 (also known as the 12.8cm PaK 44 or 80, the latter having the maximum barrel elevation limited to +15° as it was not directed to the field artillery role) was 55 calibres long, slightly shorter than that for the anti-aircraft gun, and a pepperpot muzzle brake was added to alleviate the considerable recoil forces generated on firing. The K 44 was a powerful anti-tank weapon, as its armour-penetrating projectile could penetrate 187mm (7.36in) of armour at 1,500m (1,640yd), but such was the need for artillery by 1944 most were deployed as field guns with a useful anti-armour performance.

Thankfully for the Allied armies, their constant air raids on the main centre of K 44 production at Breslau severely limited the numbers manufactured

and delivered. Two units had been completed by the end of 1943 while 1944 output was limited to just 118, with another 30 in 1945. By 1945 there were plans to place 12.8cm K 44 barrels on several types of captured French or Soviet artillery carriage, but few were produced. There was also a plan to place the 15cm sFH 18 field howitzer ordnance on the same carriage as the K 44. The result would have been the 15cm sFH 44, but none materialised before the war ended.

Specification		
Calibre:	128mm	5.04in
Length of piece:	7,023mm	276.5in
Weight travelling:	not found recorded	
Weight in action:	10,160kg	22,350lb
Traverse:	360°	
Elevation, firing:	-7.8 to +45.5°	
Muzzle velocity:	920m/s	3,018ft/sec
Max range:	24,414m	26,709yd
Shell weight:	28.3kg	62.4lb

The Krupp version of the 12.8cm K 44

Germany
15cm Kanone 16

A 15cm K 16 between the wars

a heavy gun designated the 15cm K 16 were somehow spirited away from the gaze of Treaty observers. Thus, when the Reichswehr was absorbed into the new Wehrmacht in 1933 they had to hand 28 examples of a heavy gun with which to train while preparing for future expansion. (The total production figure by 1918 was 214.) Despite the '16' designation, these guns were introduced into service in 1917, when they acted as counter-battery weapons, considered as among the best available in their class. In fact Krupp had tried to introduce such a gun as early as 1908 but there were doubts then as to its necessity, and its mobility was suspect.

In common with many other comparable artillery pieces of the time, including a similar Rheinmetall-Borsig model, the Krupp K 16 was a large and heavy weapon, so heavy that for all but the shortest moves the barrel had to be withdrawn from the carriage and carried on special transporter axles. Towing was normally by special Daimler 60hp tractors but horse teams could be used. By 1945 many K 16s had been modified for towing by half-tracked tractors. Long-distance moves had to be carried out over railways.

In 1939 the K 16 was still regarded as a front-line weapon, with all 28 examples (along with 26,100 rounds) standing ready for the invasion of Poland and subsequent campaigns. Despite their age they remained useful long-range guns as the 42-calibre barrel fired a 51.4kg (113.3lb) high-explosive projectile to a maximum range of 22,000m (24,064yd). Their bulk and weight meant they were gradually retained only as reserve weapons, and

Although the terms of the 1919 Treaty of Versailles prohibited the newly formed German Reichswehr from owning heavy artillery, numbers of

A 15cm K 16 in action on the ranges

eventually for training duties. During 1940 the number of K 16s in German service was increased by the capture of a small batch of Belgian guns originally handed over as war reparations after 1919. By 1945 there were still 16 15cm K 16 guns in service. Their non-standard 149.3mm (5.878in) ammunition (the K 16 was the only post-1939 German gun firing this calibre) was placed back into production during 1940 and remained so until 1942. As described in the following entry, the replacement for the K16 was supposed to be the 15cm K 18.

Specification		
Calibre:	149.3mm	5.878in
Length of piece:	6,410mm	252.3in
Weight travelling:	17,372kg	38,298lb
Weight in action:	10,870kg	23,964lb
Traverse:	8°	
Elevation, firing:	-3 to +42°	
Muzzle velocity:	757m/s	2,484ft/sec
Max range:	22,000m	24,064yd
Shell weight:	51.4kg	113.3lb

Germany
15cm Kanone 18

The carriage of the 15cm K 18 in the travelling position

The 15cm Kanone 18 was not one of Rheinmetall-Borsig's best ordnance products on several counts. It was originally ordered as the eventual replacement for the 15cm K 16 (see previous entry) during 1933 but the first examples did not materialise until 1938. It was an enlarged version of the heavy 10.5cm (4.14in) K 18 gun (another relative failure) and proved to be an expensive gun to manufacture, while the time-consuming feature of removing the barrel as a separate load during moves was carried over. The result was a gun that was heavier than the K 16, and

The gun-barrel transporter for the 15cm K 18 in the travelling position

just as cumbersome, but demonstrating only a marginal increase in range for all the efforts involved. In addition the projectile was lighter, although a base-fuzed anti-concrete projectile was developed. Not surprisingly, Wehrmacht ordnance officers were not particularly impressed, so the 15cm K 18 was procured in relatively small numbers only, and then at a leisurely rate. Only three guns were ready for the Polish campaign of 1939 and by 1943 only 101 had been manufactured. Production then ceased. Ammunition production ceased the year after.

The K 18 did have one unusual feature in that it had a two-piece firing table. During moves this was carried slung under the carriage. At the firing position the table was lowered to the ground and held in place by steel pickets, after which the carriage was towed up and onto the platform by one of the gun's two half-tracked tractors. The barrel was then inserted into its firing position on the carriage cradle, using ramps on each side of the carriage. Once on the platform the gun then had a steady platform and a full 360° traverse potential – on-carriage traverse was limited to a total of 11°.

All the pre-firing preparation took time and effort, so the gun was not exactly popular with its crews, although those delivered remained in service as divisional artillery pieces until the war ended – by then there were just 21 left. The K 18 had a long and slender 55-calibre barrel, firing a 43kg (94.8lb) projectile to a range of 24,500m (26,800yd). Guns issued to divisions manning the Atlantic Wall proved to be far more amenable to the coast artillery role than most field pieces as, once emplaced, their firing platforms enabled them to track naval targets.

Specification		
Calibre:	149.1mm	5.87in
Length of piece:	8,200mm	322.8in
Weight travelling:	18,700kg	41,225lb
Weight in action:	12,760kg	28,135lb
Traverse:	360 or 11°	
Elevation, firing:	-2 to +43°	
Muzzle velocity:	890m/s	2,920ft/sec
Max range:	24,500m	26,800yd
Shell weight:	43kg	94.8lb

Germany
15cm Kanone 39

The heavy gun that was to become the 15cm Kanone 39 was never intended for German army service. It was a Krupp commercial export product developed from 1938 onwards to meet an order from the Turkish army. Only two completed examples were delivered before hostilities began during September 1939, and the remainder could not be delivered. During late 1939 the German army purchased (at great expense) those guns already completed and ordered a further batch, making the

The 15cm K 39 intended for Turkey but never delivered

total acquired 64, the last 13 being manufactured and delivered during 1942.

Once in German service the gun became the 15cm Kanone 39 and was unusual in having been designed as a dual-purpose field- or coast-artillery gun. This latter role was indicated by the provision of a circular prefabricated steel platform carried as a separate load and assembled once at the firing position. Once assembled the platform was held firmly in place by steel pickets. When the gun was lifted onto the platform the split trail legs were joined together to rest on a small hand-cranked trolley onto which the trail spades were lifted. One gunner could then turn the entire gun and carriage through a full 360° traverse with little effort, enabling naval targets to be tracked with ease. In this coastal defence configuration the on-carriage traverse was limited to 6°. For the field role the split trails provided a 60° traverse, while, for moves across rough terrain, the carriage was equipped with a leaf-spring suspension. The 55-calibre barrel was essentially the same as that used for the 15cm K 18 (see previous entry) and fired much the same ammunition, although special high-explosive and armour-piercing projectiles (two types) were developed to meet Turkish requirements, the latter primarily intended for firing against warships.

This 'Turkish' ammunition was taken into German service and used until stocks were consumed. K 18 ammunition was then issued. Also as with the K 18, the K 39 barrel had to be carried as a separate load during moves, making three loads with the prefabricated platform and more for the ammunition. The extra logistics loads seem to have been tolerated, especially as it seems that most K 39s, from 1941 onwards, were assigned to the coastal defence role, where their weight handicaps would no longer be troublesome.

Specification		
Calibre:	149.1mm	5.87in
Length of piece:	8,250mm	324.8in
Weight travelling:	18,282kg	40,304lb
Weight in action:	12,186kg	28,809lb
Traverse:	360 or 60°	
Elevation, firing:	-3 to +46°	
Muzzle velocity:	865m/s	2,838ft/sec
Max range:	24,700m	27,000yd
Shell weight:	43kg	94.8lb

Germany
15cm SchiffsKanone SK C/28

15cm SchiffsKanone SK C/28 in travelling configuration

The inclusion of a naval gun in a summary of heavy artillery is brought about by the fact that, from the early development stages onwards the designers', Rheinmetall-Borsig, far-sightedly intended the end result to be an all-purpose weapon. While the original naval gun design was in progress (paper studies began during 1928), parallel developments for both static and mobile coastal defence guns were also in progress. As was usual with Rheinmetall-Borsig, development was careful and thorough, so the mobile coastal defence variant emerged as an advanced and highly mobile gun that could equally well be employed as a field-artillery piece despite the carriage's relative bulk and weight.

The SK C/28 had a barrel 55 calibres long, capable of firing a 43.5kg (99.7lb) projectile to 23,500m (25,700yd). Ammunition types developed (again primarily for the coastal defence role, none of them compatible with other field artillery munitions of the same calibre) included concrete or armour-piercing, and high-explosive, impact- or delayed-action-fuzed. After early proposals to tow the gun in three loads, the combined gun and carriage eventually became a unitary load on two twin-axle bogies, one at each end, spreading the wheel pressures over eight pneumatic tyres. Once at a firing position, the central carriage and firing platform were lowered to the ground with two outrigger leg stabilisers folded down each side.

As the mobile version of the SK C/28 was supposed to be deployed primarily as a coastal defence gun, it had provision for loading assistance systems and centralised fire control. Such refinements were not strictly needed in a field setting, but from time to time the SK C/28 was deployed in the field role, especially on the Eastern Front, where long-range artillery was always at a premium. For the land campaigns the guns continued to be crewed by their original German navy personnel.

There was one further role for the 15cm SK C/28 ordnance to play. During 1941, with the invasion of

the Soviet Union pending, eight 21cm Mrs 18 (qv) carriages were standing idle due to delays in barrel production. Eight spare SK C/28 barrels were therefore installed on those carriages and sent East. They were employed only until the intended 21cm (8.3in) howitzer barrels became available. The SK C/28 barrels were then removed from their carriages, to be replaced by the intended ordnance. The entire exercise provided but one indication of the Germans' desperate need for long-range heavy artillery from 1941 onwards.

Specification		
Calibre:	149.1mm	5.87in
Length of piece:	8,291mm	364.4in
Weight travelling:	26,163kg	57,678lb
Weight in action:	19,761kg	43,565lb
Traverse:	360°	
Elevation, firing:	-7.5 to +47.5°	
Muzzle velocity:	875m/s	2,870ft/sec
Max range:	23,500m	25,700yd
Shell weight:	43.5kg	99.7lb

Germany
17cm Kanone 18 in Mörserlafette

By 1939 Wehrmacht artillery planners had already determined that their existing 15cm heavy guns could not provide the ballistic and mobility performances that the future would demand, so Krupp were asked to develop and manufacture an entirely modern piece to replace them. The Krupp solution, the 17cm Kanone 18 in Mörserlafette, was introduced into service during 1941, sharing the same innovative carriage as the 21cm Mörser 18 (qv). This carriage operated on the dual-recoil system, where the barrel recoil mechanisms operated as usual, with stresses on the carriage further reduced almost to zero by a gun platform sliding to the rear along rails on the box trail. Another novelty was that once in position a firing platform was jacked down to lift the carriage wheels off the ground. As well as forming a very steady firing platform, the carriage was then so

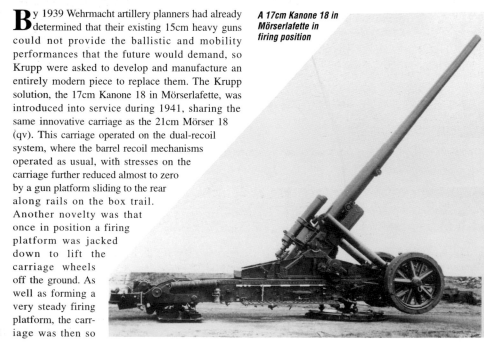

A 17cm Kanone 18 in Mörserlafette in firing position

balanced that two gunners could traverse the gun through a full 360° traverse with relative ease. For transport over all but the very shortest distances the K 18 had to be carried in two loads, although the design detail was such that combining and separating the two loads involved a minimum of time and labour.

From the outset the 17cm K 18 proved to be a great success, soon becoming the mainstay of the German heavy-artillery batteries. The 50-calibre barrel fired a 68kg (149.9lb) projectile to no less than 29,600m (32,382yd). The K 18 was soon in great demand but production at the Hanomag works at Hanover, despite being assigned the highest production priority, was constantly disrupted by Allied air raids, so much so that by the time the war ended the total produced was only 338, well below requirements. Only 40 were manufactured during the whole of 1944, a year when they were sorely needed. By the time the war ended only 88 were still in action.

One unusual aspect of the ammunition for a gun of this calibre was the provision of a 71kg (156.5lb) armour-piercing projectile in the ammunition suite. This was primarily intended for direct fire against tanks, although by the time tanks appeared anywhere near K 18 gun positions, something would already have gone very wrong. It is interesting to note that during late 1944 and 1945 US army gunners were happy to turn captured 17cm K 18s against their former owners.

Specification		
Calibre:	172.5mm	6.79in
Length of piece:	8,529.5mm	335.8in
Weight travelling:	23,375kg	51,532lb
Weight in action:	17,510kg	38,602lb
Traverse:	360 or 16°	
Elevation, firing:	0 to +50°	
Muzzle velocity:	925m/s	3,035ft/sec
Max range:	29,600m	32,382yd
Shell weight:	68kg	149.9lb

A 17cm Kanone 18 in Mörserlafette emplaced as a coastal defence gun

Germany
21cm Kanone 38

Almost as soon as the 21cm Mrs 18 (qv) had been introduced into service Krupp were requested to develop a 210mm (8.27in) gun with comparable mobility to be installed on a similar Mörserlafette carriage, the intention being that it would replace the Mrs 18, which was thought to be lacking in range. The result was the 21cm K 38,

ordered in 1938. The K 38 ordnance was based on a Krupp 1936 export design having a 55.5-calibre barrel, placed on a dual-recoil carriage similar to that used for the 21cm Mrs 18, but with many significant refinements introduced following experience with the earlier designs. One was a system of inclined surfaces, pulleys and hand winches that considerably reduced the time and workload involved in getting the heavy gun and carriage in and out of action (the gun travelled in two loads plus a stores vehicle).

Once in action the gun rested on a firing platform under the carriage providing a full 360° traverse when the trails were lifted and moved by two of the crew. Once in action a 120kg (264lb) projectile could be fired to a range of 33,900m (36,950yd). Only one projectile, a high-explosive, appears to have been manufactured for the K 38.

At first German artillery personnel were very impressed by the K 38, but they gradually came to consider that the power of the gun, as good as it was, was insufficient to justify all the personnel, manufacturing and resource demands involved. In addition, production at Essen was slow.

Of the original 16 ordered for delivery during 1940 only one had been completed by 1941. A further six had been completed before an order was issued in May 1942 to discontinue production in favour of other,

A 21cm K 38 barrel ready to move

The carriage for the 21cm K 38 in the travelling configuration

higher-priority needs, although at one stage there were plans for Krupp to manufacture 60, with the Skodawerke at Pilsen contributing a further 40. Of the seven examples completed none remained in service by the Fall of 1944, all having been captured or destroyed on the Eastern Front, while one complete equipment was shipped to Japan. Exactly why this happened is now not clear. It is not even known if the gun ever got to Japan. From a purely technical point of view, many observers continue to regard the 21cm K 38 as the finest German artillery design of its period.

Specification		
Calibre:	210.9mm	8.3in
Length of piece:	11,620mm	457.5in
Weight travelling:	34,825kg	76,775lb
Weight in action:	25,435kg	55,957lb
Traverse:	360 or 18°	
Elevation, firing:	0 to +50°	
Muzzle velocity:	905m/s	2,968ft/sec
Max range:	33,900m	36,950yd
Shell weight:	120kg	264lb

Germany
24cm Kanone 3

The long barrel of the 24cm K 3 looming above Aberdeen Proving Ground in the USA

During the 1920s, Reichswehr staff officers analysing the tactical findings from the Great War years that resulted in the '18' class of artillery designs, rounded off their findings by requesting a 240mm (actual calibre 238mm/9.38in) long-range gun. The project was accorded a low priority, as other artillery needs were judged more important, so although design work by Rheinmetall-Borsig started during 1934 the first example did not appear until 1939. The resultant 24cm K 3 was one of the more remarkable (and complex) guns to appear during the war years.

Its 54.6-calibre barrel appeared to be too long for the carriage, another enlarged version of the dual-recoil Mörserlafette used for the 17cm K 18 (qv). The barrel and ammunition combination enabled a 152.3kg (335lb) projectile to be fired to a maximum range of 37,500m (40,875yd) but this remarkable performance had to be paid for, and it was paid for mainly in weight. The size and bulk of the K 3 was such that it had to be transported in six loads, including a generator that provided electrical power to assist in assembling the gun once at a firing position.

Assembly took 90 minutes and involved a team of 25 gunners, although was still far less than for any comparable equipment, while the rate of fire was one round every three to four minutes.

Only ten K 3s were manufactured (by Krupp, not Rheinmetall-Borsig, for some reason), the last two being delivered during 1944. They were issued to a single heavy-artillery regiment, organised into three batteries, each with two guns. The K 3 was also employed for a great deal of experimentation, including a 'squeeze-bore' muzzle attachment that fired experimental projectiles (with a final calibre of 180mm/7.08in) to a range of 60,000m (65,617yd). Wehrmacht ordnance officers considered that, despite all the K 3's remarkable performance, it provided too short a range for all the cost, complexity and installation time involved.

Following their experiences manufacturing and testing the K 3, Krupp proposed a 24cm K 4, which would have a 72-calibre barrel firing a 160kg (352lb) projectile to 49,000m (53,587yd) and would be carried into action slung between two turretless Tiger tank chassis. Work did commence on the K 4 project but Allied bombers intervened and destroyed the developmental hardware before it was completed. The K 4 project was then dropped.

Specification		
Calibre:	238mm	9.38in
Length of piece:	13,104mm	515.9in
Weight travelling:	84,836kg	187,0281lb
Weight in action:	54,000kg	119,000lb
Traverse:	360 or 6°	
Elevation, firing:	-1 to +56°	
Muzzle velocity:	870m/s	2,850ft/sec
Max range:	37,500m	40,875yd
Shell weight:	152.3kg	335lb

Germany
15cm schwere Feldhaubitze 13

The 15cm schwere Feldhaubitze 13 was introduced into limited German service during 1913 as the replacement for a similar but shorter-barrelled model, the 15cm sFH 02. It was not produced in any numbers until 1917, and by the time the Great War ended, 696 had been manufactured by Krupp. The survivors were all supposed to be handed over to the Allies under the terms of the Treaty of Versailles, but, as with many other German weapons, an undetermined number was carefully hidden away from Treaty observers' scrutiny to be occasionally used for clandestine training. Some war reparation examples were handed over to Belgium and The Netherlands, who retained them until 1940.

After 1933 these howitzers were employed mainly for training, as their ballistic performance, although very acceptable for the Great War period, was considered to be nowhere near what was required. In addition to having a range of only 8,600m (8,408yd) with a 40.8kg (89.96lb) projectile from the 17-calibre barrel, they were originally designed for horse traction in one unwieldy load and proved to be unsuitable for conversion to mechanical traction. They were therefore relegated to non-age-related tasks such as firing shells for trainee artillery observers to spot. By 1939 the 15cm sFH 13 no longer featured in German weapon holding reports.

A change came during 1940, when the Dutch and Belgian war reparation howitzers returned to the German fold, along with stocks of ammunition, raising the sFH 13 gun park total considerably. There were too many to overlook for potential active service, but they fired different calibre (149.7mm/5.89in) ammunition to other German howitzers, the production of which had ceased in 1918, while the lack of mobility factor remained. A use was found for these antiques by converting them for the self-propelled artillery role. During 1942, 102 howitzers were placed on captured French Chenilette Lorraine tracked utility carrier chassis by Alfred Becker of Krefeld to provide a stopgap measure of mobile artillery fire support for Panzer divisions. All available ammunition was issued to these batteries; once consumed there would be no more.

Some examples of the self-propelled conversion, the SdKfz 135/1, saw action in North Africa, and 17 were still around in France in 1944. Reports mention that others served on the Eastern Front. None survived in service by 1945.

Specification		
Calibre:	149.7mm	5.89in
Length of piece:	2,550mm	100.4in
Weight travelling (approx):	3,000kg	6,615lb
Weight in action:	2,250kg	4,961lb
Traverse:	9°	
Elevation, firing:	-5 to +45°	
Muzzle velocity:	381m/s	1,250ft/sec
Max range:	8,600m	8,408yd
Shell weight:	40.8kg	89.96lb

Germany
15cm schwere Feldhaubitze 18 and 18M

A 15cm sFH 18 captured on the Eastern Front

The 15cm schwere Feldhaubitze 18 and 15cm Kanone 18 (qv) were developed side by side from 1926 to 1930 and shared the same carriage. It was a combined effort, the 29.6-calibre ordnance coming from Rheinmetall-Borsig and the carriage from Krupp. Production had already started by 1933 and thereafter the 15cm sFH 18 served as the backbone of the German field and heavy artillery formations. By 1944 the howitzer was in series production at four main centres, with component manufacturers adding more, and the combined totals were prodigious by German standards (although the demands for replacements and for newly formed formations were never fully met). Between 1939 and the end of the war no fewer than 5,403 examples had been manufactured and they served on all Fronts.

The 15cm sFH 18 was a good, sound design using a steady, split-trail carriage providing a wide angle of traverse (64°), and fired a useful 43.5kg (95.7lb) high-explosive projectile to a maximum of 13,250m

(14,490yd). However, its maximum practical range was limited to 9,725m (10,635yd), as using the two top charges introduced after 1942 caused excessive barrel and chamber erosion, shortening their practical service life, so its employment was limited to special-fire missions. A late-1942 development introduced a replaceable barrel liner and a slotted muzzle brake to alleviate the erosion problem. This created the 15cm sFH 18M, but the restrictions on firing with the top two charges remained.

The sFH 18 displayed the usual '18' artillery design features of the recoil and recuperator housings being located over and under the barrel for easy replacement when necessary. Many types of projectile were developed for the sFH 18 and sFH 18M including, for the latter, a rocket-assisted projectile with an intended range of 19,000m (20,778yd). However, the projectile proved to be inaccurate and difficult to manufacture, so it was little used. Another projectile had a shaped charge warhead for the direct-fire, anti-armour role. Towing as one load by both horses and vehicles was possible. The 15cm sFH 18 was deployed in the self-propelled artillery role as the Hummel (Bumble Bee), 714 of which were produced between 1943 and 1945. In 1939 Finland was provided with 48 15cm sFH 18s, and more were passed to Italy. After 1945 the sFH 18 continued to serve with several European armies for many years.

Specification		
Calibre:	149mm	5.87in
Length of piece:	4,440mm	174.8in
Weight travelling (approx):	3,000kg	6,615lb
Weight in action:	5,512kg	12,154lb
Traverse:	64°	
Elevation, firing:	-3 to +45°	
Muzzle velocity (max):	520m/s	1,710ft/sec
Max range:	13,325m	14,490yd
Shell weight:	43.5kg	95.7lb

A 15cm sFH 18 in action on the Western Front, Winter 1939/40

Germany
15cm schwere Feldhaubitze 36

The 15cm schwere Feldhaubitze 36 was the result of a German army requirement issued during 1935 for a lighter version of the 15cm sFH 18 (see previous entry) capable of being towed by a single horse team – the sFH 18 could be horse-drawn but was more suited to mechanical traction. The intention was to provide lighter howitzers for infantry, cavalry and other divisions where there was little, if any, motorised transport. Rheinmetall-Borsig were awarded the development contract and designed what became known as the 15cm sFH 36.

The sFH 36 ordnance emerged as lighter and slightly longer that that of the sFH 18, and sported a muzzle brake to reduce firing stresses inflicted on the split-trail carriage. For the carriage the Rheinmetall-Borsig designers made extensive use of light aluminium alloys in order to save weight. The sFH 36 fired the same ammunition suite as the sFH 18 but the number of propellant charges was reduced from eight to seven, reducing the maximum possible range compared to the sFH 18 in the process.

By 1939 the 15cm sFH 36 was considered as suitable for service pending final trials, and production preparations were being made, when all further work ceased for two main reasons. One was that as early as 1939 German war planners began to appreciate that their stocks of raw materials for weapon production were not as high as intended, with aluminium being in particularly short supply. At that time the Luftwaffe had production priority over the army and navy, so all supplies of aluminium had to be reserved for them. The second reason was the sFH 36 became ready for production at a time when production facilities were at a premium. Any attempt to get the sFH 36 into production could only be at the cost of disrupting other badly needed weapons. The end result was that the sFH 36 was withdrawn from production almost as soon as it began, the handful of completed guns soon being withdrawn as non-standard weapons creating logistic problems.

There is no mention of the sFH 36 in German service holdings from when the war began in September 1939. The ordnance development work was not completely wasted, for it was used as the basis for the 15cm sFH 42 and the 15cm sFH 18/40.

Specification		
Calibre:	149mm	5.87in
Length of piece:	3,805mm	149.8in
Weight travelling (approx):	3,500kg	7,716lb
Weight in action:	3,280kg	7,232lb
Traverse:	56°	
Elevation, firing:	0 to +45°	
Muzzle velocity (max):	485m/s	1,591ft/sec
Max range:	12,300m	13,450yd
Shell weight:	43.5kg	95.7lb

The short-lived sFH 36 with its muzzle brake prominent

Germany
15cm schwere Feldhaubitze 18/40 (42)

As good as the 15cm sFH 18 was for its period, the German army, as ever, still wanted something better in maximum range terms. In 1938 they issued a formal requirement for a heavy field howitzer with a range of over 15,000m (16,404yd) and the ability to fire at elevation angles up to +70°. Krupp and Rheinmetall-Borsig designed essentially similar solutions, both appearing during 1941, with the result that Rheinmetall-Borsig once again concentrated on the ordnance and Krupp on the light steel carriage. Rheinmetall-Borsig based their ordnance design on that for the unfortunate 15cm sFH 36 (see previous entry), complete with a similar slotted muzzle brake, but increased in length to 32.5 calibres and with a barrel liner that could be replaced when worn or eroded.

The result, the 15cm schwere Feldhaubitze 40, provided the required range increase using existing sFH 18 family ammunition and was deemed ready for production, only to run into one of the obstacles already encountered when sFH 36 production was planned. The sFH 40 could only be introduced at the expense of severely disrupting existing facilities for the current production of other sorely needed items, so the sFH 40 programme was terminated. By that stage Rheinmetall-Borsig had already manufactured

The long-range but ill-starred 15cm sFH 18/40

46 barrels, so they were placed on standard 15cm sFH 18 carriages and issued as the 15cm sFH 18/40. In service the barrel and carriage combination proved to be less accurate than the sFH 18/40, and the carriage prevented elevation angles above +45°. The hybrid was therefore not greatly favoured, despite the increase in maximum range, but had to be retained, such was the shortage of serviceable field howitzers. By February 1945 only 24 were left.

From 1943 onwards, demands for more and better equipments were constantly arriving from all Fronts. It was therefore decided that the 15cm sFH 18/40 would be placed back into production under the revised designation of 15cm sFH 42. Production was planned to be carried out at the same four main facilities as the sFH 18, but it never began, all the facilities continuing to concentrate on the production of existing weapons. The sFH 42 was meant to be only a stopgap measure pending the introduction of the 15cm sFH 43, basically an updated sFH 18 barrel on a 360° traverse cruciform carriage. The sFH 43 project never got past the wooden-mock-up stage before the war ended.

Specification		
Calibre:	149mm	5.87in
Length of piece:	4,875mm	191.3in
Weight travelling:	6,480kg	14,288lb
Weight in action:	5,720kg	12,613lb
Traverse:	56°	
Elevation, firing:	0 to +45°	
Muzzle velocity (max):	595m/s	1,952ft/sec
Max range:	15,100m	16,514yd
Shell weight:	43.5kg	95.7lb

Germany
Langer 21cm Mörser

The term 'langer', in langer 21cm Mörser, was the term applied when the howitzer was first introduced by Krupp during 1916, denoting that the new howitzer had a longer barrel than the 12-calibre 21cm howitzer it was meant to replace. The new howitzer had a 14.6-calibre barrel which increased the maximum range potential only slightly compared to its predecessor, but otherwise few changes were introduced, and the new howitzer was considered successful enough for the static conditions of the Great War. As it was the most up-to-date heavy howitzer in service in 1918 all examples were earmarked for hiding away from Treaty of Versailles observers at various remote storage facilities within Germany throughout most of the 1920s. Apart from a few clandestine training exercises, there they remained until about 1930 or soon after.

Hiding them must have been a difficult undertaking because the lg 21cm Mrs was a high, bulky and awkward-looking howitzer, although, in common with the practice of its time, it could be broken down into two loads, barrel and carriage, for towing by large teams of horses. When the new Wehrmacht was formed during 1933, the old howitzer's replacement, the 21cm Mrs 18 (qv), was already planned, so the veterans were initially employed for training purposes only. By 1934/35 it was appreciated that replacement howitzers were still some years off in the future so, as a stopgap precaution, it was decided to modernise 28 of the old lg 21cm Mrs by updating their carriages.

Once the necessary modifications had been introduced the howitzer could be towed by mechanised tractors as a single load carried on a limber and new, rubber-tyred steel wheels. The original shield was removed and some other detail

changes were introduced. In 1939 the lg 21cm Mrs was still a front-line equipment, although recognised as obsolete, and remained so until at least 1942, after which the survivors were retired and returned to training duties.

Despite its age the lg 21cm Mrs could fire a useful 113kg (249lb) high-explosive or 121.4kg (267.7lb) concrete-penetrating projectile (the projectiles were the same as those fired by the 21cm Mrs 18, its eventual replacement) but its maximum range was limited to 11,100m (12,139yd), too short by modern warfare standards, considering the weight and awkward handling involved.

Specification		
Calibre:	210.9mm	8.31in
Length of piece:	3,063mm	120.6in
Weight travelling:	11,257kg	24,817lb
Weight in action:	9,220kg	20,330lb
Traverse:	4°	
Elevation, firing:	+6 to +70°	
Muzzle velocity (max):	393m/s	1,289ft/sec
Max range:	11,100m	12,143yd
Shell weight:	113kg	249lb

A surviving example of a 21cm Mrs acting as a gate guardian

Germany
21cm Mörser 18

Development of the 21cm Mörser 18 began at Krupp during 1933 and continued alongside that of the 17cm Kanone 18 (qv). Both pieces shared the same innovative, dual-recoil carriage, although the carriage for the Mrs 18 had its maximum

elevation angle increased to +70°. For a period after 1939 the production of guns and howitzers went ahead with the same priority, but gradually gunners expressed a preference for the significantly longer-ranged 17cm K 18, despite the lighter projectile 51

A 21cm Mrs 18 ready for the road

fired. Production quantities reflected this preference until 1941, when production of the Mrs 18 ceased altogether in favour of the gun. By that time 500 examples of the Mrs 18 had been completed and delivered.

However, the demands for heavy artillery continued and became so strident that, as production tooling was still available, it was decided to put the 21cm Mrs 18 back into production again during 1943. Production facilities at Hanomag at Hanover and Krupp at Essen were re-established with a minimum of disruption, and production then continued at both centres until April 1945, by which time a further 211 examples had been completed.

This raised the 21cm Mrs 18's production total to 711, far exceeding that for the 17cm K 18 and reversing the gunners' original preferences.

The 21cm Mrs 18 served on all Fronts and proved to be a sound, reliable howitzer. It had a 31-calibre barrel, rather long for a howitzer of the period, so it could fire a 113kg (249lb) high-explosive projectile to a range of 18,900m (20,670yd). There was also a concrete-piercing projectile weighing 121.4kg (267.6lb). The Mrs 18 was one of the few operational artillery equipments cleared to fire the top secret, fin-stabilised Röchling Granate, with its spectacular concrete or masonry penetration capabilities. Although 9,920 examples of the latter

A trio of 21cm Mrs 18s captured by the Soviets on the Eastern Front

projectile were manufactured, at great expense, they were little used operationally for fears of their secrets falling into Allied hands. No performance data regarding them seems to have survived.

Thanks to its high elevation angle the 21cm Mrs 18 could effectively cover a very wide range band, the minimum range being 3,000m (3,281yd). For long moves the Mrs 18 was split into two loads for towing by half-tracked tractors. Carriages with one rubber-tyred wheel on each side or two pneumatic-tyred wheels per side were manufactured.

Specification		
Calibre:	210.9mm	8.31in
Length of piece:	6,510mm	256.3in
Weight travelling (approx):	22,700kg	50,045lb
Weight in action:	16,700kg	36,824lb
Traverse:	360 or 16°	
Elevation, firing:	0 to +70°	
Muzzle velocity (max):	565m/s	1,854ft/sec
Max range:	18,900m	20,670yd
Shell weight:	113kg	249lb

Germany
28cm Haubitze L/12

The stubby barrel of the 28cm Haubitze L/12 on its special transporter

For the origins of the 28cm Haubitze L/12 it is necessary to look back to the 1880s and 1890s when consideration was first given to the defeat of the concrete-protected fortifications then being built all over Europe. The artillery solution seemed to be deep-penetrating projectiles with delayed-action fuzes to produce detonation after penetration, and near-vertical final trajectories – the larger the calibre, the better. One of the results of this philosophy was a 280mm (11.14in) heavy howitzer from Krupp, the German army acquiring a quantity as the 28cm Haubitze L/12. A similar design, the

28cm Küsten Haubitze, was also adopted for coastal defence. As both these howitzers were intended for static warfare, little consideration was given to mobility other than the option to transport them in several loads to a firing position where they could be left for prolonged periods. It took from three to four days to install a 28cm H L/12, and just as long to remove it again.

The 28cm H L/12 was deployed between 1914 and 1918, at least one being returned to the Krupp works at Essen, where it remained when the Armistice intervened. It seems a safe conjecture that it survived destruction under the terms of the Treaty of Versailles by being disguised as a 28cm Küsten Haubitze, the retention of which was allowed as a legal coastal defence howitzer. That single example survived at Essen until 1942, when the howitzer was refurbished and sent east, by railway, to take part in the attack on Sevastopol, along with two 28cm Küsten Haubitze. The refurbishment meant that several half-tracks had to be diverted from their normal duties to tow the various loads to their firing position using updated transporter trailers.

After the fall of Sevastopol the H L/12 went back to Germany, where it served as a device for the development of bagged propellant charges. The H L/12 was by then the only weapon in the German armoury that still used bagged charges, all other in-service artillery equipments (even the 28cm Küsten Haubitze) utilising costly brass or steel cartridge case obturation at a time when raw material shortages were becoming critical. Nothing emerged from the H L/12 trials other than the intention to utilise bagged charges on future designs whenever possible.

Specification		
Calibre:	283mm	11.14in
Length of piece:	3,396mm	133.7in
Weight travelling:	not found recorded	
Weight in action:	50,300kg	110,890lb
Traverse:	360°	
Elevation, firing:	0 to +65°	
Muzzle velocity (max):	350m/s	1,148ft/sec
Max range:	10,400m	11,370yd
Shell weight:	350kg	770lb

Germany
35.5cm Haubitze Mörser 1 (M1)

In this illustration the gun crew provides an indication of the scale of the 35.5cm Haubitze Mörser 1 (M1)

As with other German heavy artillery groupings, the 24cm K 3 gun had a howitzer counterpart sharing the same dual-recoil carriage design. It was the 35.5cm Haubitze Mörser (M1), developed alongside the 24cm K 3 by Rheinmetall-Borsig in response to a German army requirement dated 1935. As with the K 4, development of the H M1 was protracted, not least by the imperative to concentrate on more pressing requirements, so it was not until 1939 that the first example appeared. It emerged as a massive piece of artillery but one with many advanced features. It carried over the field assembly methods of the K 3 in that a series of ramps, handling devices and winches were used to get the seven transport loads, all pulled by half-tracks, into a single unit ready to fire. One of the loads was an electrical generator that not only provided power for a crane gantry during assembly but also provided the power for barrel elevation and traverse once in action. Time into action was two hours, a considerable achievement when compared to previous designs. The firepower of the H M1 was considerable. It fired a 575kg (1,267.6lb) projectile to a maximum of 20,850m (22,800yd) and could also fire the special Röchling-Granate 42 concrete-penetrating projectile weighing no less than 926kg (2,041lb) – few of the latter were employed operationally.

After 1939, production at Düsseldorf continued at a sedate pace, for it was not until 1942 that the next example appeared – five were manufactured that year. The 1943 output was just one, with the last example following in 1944, making a total of just eight completed (plus some spare barrels). Further planned production was terminated when it was realised that these massive howitzers absorbed too many scarce raw materials in return for a few specialised fire missions. Projectile production alone was a considerable undertaking, 3,921

standard (not Röchling) concrete-piercing projectiles being manufactured at great expense.

There was only one artillery battalion employing these heavy howitzers and that had just two single H M1 howitzer batteries, the howitzers no doubt being allotted on a rotating basis. The H M1 saw action during the attack on Sevastopol and also took part in the Siege of Leningrad, where at least one was lost when the siege was finally lifted.

Specification		
Calibre:	355.6mm	14in
Length of piece:	10,265mm	404.13in
Weight travelling (approx):	123,500kg	272,266lb
Weight in action (approx):	78,000kg	171,957lb
Traverse:	360 or 6°	
Elevation, firing:	+45 to +75°	
Muzzle velocity (max):	570m/s	1,870ft/sec
Max range:	20,850m	22,800yd
Shell weight:	575kg	1,267.6lb

Germany
42cm Gamma-Mörser

In 1905 Krupp were asked to design and develop what was then regarded as the ultimate in fortress smashers, a 420mm (16.53in) super-heavy howitzer. Krupp, rightly sensing lucrative contracts, responded

with a total of ten complete howitzers and 18 spare barrels by 1918. One model, the 42cm Dicke Bertha (Big Bertha), was placed on an enormous semi-mobile field-mounting to smash the Belgian forts around Liège in 1914. Another model, the Gamma-Mörser, with a 16-calibre barrel, was more static, firing from a fixed platform against the well-protected Verdun forts in 1916, although with less effect than against the Liège forts.

The 42cm Gamma-Mörser in splendid isolation on the Meppen ranges

After 1918 all surviving models except one were either destroyed or reduced to scrap. The sole survivor was one of the fixed-platform Gamma-Mörser that had ended the war on Krupp's private firing range at Meppen, apparently being used at one stage for the development of concrete-penetrating projectiles. It seems to have survived after 1918 mainly because it was too much trouble for Treaty observers to move away, so it was still at Meppen in 1940. There are indications that some measures were then under consideration to somehow make the monster more mobile to tackle the French Maginot Line forts, but they fell without the intervention of the Gamma-Mörser. It remained at Meppen until 1942 when it was dismantled into a series of loads by a team of 285 soldiers and loaded onto nine special railway flatbed wagons (plus a further carriage for stores and personnel) and moved east to the Crimea. Once there, and following considerable labour and an installation period of nearly three days, the Gamma-Mörser fired into the beleaguered city of Sevastopol with great effect and alongside the rest of the specially assembled German siege train. Each concrete-penetrating projectile weighed a hefty 1,020kg (2,249lb), base-fuzed to ensure the 91kg (200lb) high-explosive payload detonated only when well inside the target structure. Maximum range was 14,200m (15,530yd).

Once the city had fallen the Gamma-Mörser was uprooted once again and taken back to Meppen. Exactly what happened to the Gamma-Mörser after then is uncertain. There are reports it was in operation during the Warsaw Rising of 1944 but these cannot be confirmed and seem unlikely. Ammunition for the Gamma-Mörser was still being manufactured as late as 1943, 1,391 projectiles having been manufactured between 1940 and then.

Specification		
Calibre:	420mm	16.53in
Length of piece:	6,724mm	264.7in
Weight travelling:	not found recorded	
Weight in action (approx):	140,000kg	308,642lb
Traverse:	46°	
Elevation, firing:	+43 to +75°	
Muzzle velocity (max):	452m/s	1,483ft/sec
Max range:	14,200m	15,530yd
Shell weight:	1,020kg	2,249lb

Germany
Gerät 040 and 041

The 54cm Gerät 041, demonstrating its imposing bulk

The Gerät 040 and 041 were the heaviest artillery equipments ever to be placed on tracked chassis, but to call them self-propelled would be stretching the point. Their weight and bulk made anything but the shortest moves under their own power impossible. Anything more than a few kilometres demanded a laborious stripping down into separate loads, while long-distance moves required railways and special railcars. Both equipments came about from a mid-1930s request for an artillery system capable of destroying any of the French Maginot Line forts, something requiring super-heavy calibres. Initial studies by Rheinmetall-Borsig included a conventional platform-type carriage, but the weights involved made such a solution so immobile it was decided to mount short howitzer barrels on enormous self-powered tracked chassis.

The first result was the Gerät 040, with a 600mm (23.6in) 8.44-calibre barrel firing a 2,170kg (4,774lb) concrete-piercing projectile to a maximum 4,500m (4,900yd) range, soon considered as too short for tactical comfort. The first of two Gerät 040s was not ready before the Fall of France in 1940, so their intended targets passed them by. Rather than the super-heavy approach becoming redundant, another six examples were manufactured at enormous cost, but these were Gerät 041s, with a 540mm (21.3in) 11.5-calibre barrel, their range increased to 10,400m (11,300yd).

Although the Gerät 041 projectile weight was reduced to 1,250kg (2,750lb), this was still more than sufficient to smash any fortification of up to 3.5m (11.5ft) of reinforced concrete, as two systems were able to demonstrate at Sevastopol in 1942. Getting those two examples to the Crimea must have been a major logistic undertaking. The tracked carriages had to be suspended between two special rail cars, and the barrel occupied another. Other wagons carried erection gantries, tools and all the other bits and pieces necessary to get the howitzer into operation. Turretless PzKpfw IV tank chassis were employed as ammunition carriers, each carrying three projectiles and having its own crane to lift the projectiles up to the loading platform.

At least one of these monsters was employed during the suppression of the Warsaw Rising of 1944 and at least two others were employed at odd times during the prolonged Siege of Leningrad. Most had been destroyed by the time the war ended, although a Gerät 040 can still be seen in a military museum near Moscow.

Specification

Calibre:	540mm	21.3in
Length of piece:	6,724mm	264.7in
Weight travelling (approx):	124,000kg	272,800lb
Weight in action (approx):	124,000kg	272,800lb
Traverse:	8°	
Elevation, firing:	0 to +70°	
Muzzle velocity (max):	387m/s	1,270ft/sec
Max range:	10,400m	11,300yd
Shell weight:	1,250kg	2,750lb

The ordnance of the 54cm Gerät 041

Italy
Cannone da 149/35 A

The very appearance of the Cannone da 149/35 A shows how outdated it was by 1940

The Cannone da 149/35 A was one of the most ancient designs still in service with the Italian army (or any other army) in 1940, having entered service in about 1902, even then based on artillery design concepts some years old. Perhaps the most obvious indication of its antiquity was that it lacked any form of recoil system, all recoil forces being absorbed by the mass of the carriage itself, large flat plates strapped around the wheels, and the gun and carriage recoiling up two long ramps placed behind the wheels. While the drama and movements involved with each firing may have impressed colonial populations with a sense of the gun's power, for the gun crews it meant having to manhandle the gun back to its original firing position after every firing, and relaying the barrel. As the carriage offered no degree of traverse control, every horizontal movement of the barrel had to be made by manually moving the entire mass using handspikes, so laying the Cannone da 149/35 A was a laborious undertaking and the resultant rate of fire was slow.

Matters were not helped by the retention of a sighting circle at a time when nearly all other artillery pieces were indirectly aimed using panoramic sights. The gun itself was originally a 38.7-calibre Armstrong design (hence the A) manufactured in Italy, with firing accomplished using a friction tube, another indication of the gun's antiquity. For all its characteristics carried over from a previous era, the Cannone da 149/35 A could still fire a 45.96kg (101.3lb) projectile to a maximum range of 16,500m (18.050yd).

By 1940 it had long been appreciated that the Cannone da 149/35 A was obsolete and there were plans to replace it with the Cannone da 149/40 modello 35 (qv). Production of the new gun was slow, so in 1940 there were still 895 of the old guns available for service. Some of the veterans saw action during the Italian army's Albanian and Greek campaigns, still firing shrapnel projectiles on occasion. By 1940 there were several sub-variants still in service, most of them with only minor modifications to the carriage and barrel rifling, some introduced as late as 1935. During 1942 there were still 64 based in North Africa. Their longevity was probably only outstripped by some of the old 1880-period artillery pieces removed from fortresses by the French army in 1914.

Specification		
Calibre:	149.1mm	5.87in
Length of piece:	5,722mm	225.3in
Weight travelling:	not found recorded	
Weight in action:	8,220kg	18,125lb
Traverse:	0°	
Elevation, firing:	-10 to +35°	
Muzzle velocity (max):	651m/s	2,136ft/sec
Max range:	16,500m	18,050yd
Shell weight:	45.96kg	101.3lb

Italy
Cannone da 149/40 modello 35

In 1934 Ansaldo produced the prototype of a new 149.1mm (5.87in) gun for the Italian army, with the intention of replacing the many elderly models still in service. The following year, and following extensive trials, the gun was accepted for service as the Cannone da 149/40 modello 35 and ordered into immediate production. The initial order was for 590 examples, although long-term plans envisaged more. It took time to establish a production line at the Ansaldo factory in Turin; so long that by September 1940 only 51 guns had been delivered, an indication not of a lack of Italian artillery design skills, but of a lack of engineering and industrial infrastructure to manufacture weapons in quantity.

As a design, the Cannone da 149/40 modello 35 was quite advanced, once the anomaly was overlooked regarding the old practice of the split trail legs being provided with extra stability during firing by hammering trail stakes into the ground at the end of each leg. Hammering in the stakes took little time but getting them out again before the carriage could be moved was a different matter. The 40.5-calibre-long barrel could fire a 46kg (101.4lb) projectile to a maximum range of 23,700m (25,928yd) at a steady firing rate of one round per minute. For normal moves the barrel and carriage formed two loads towed by Breda tractors. When operating in mountainous or close terrain the number of loads could be increased to four, making a total weight when travelling of 13,809kg (30,443lb).

From 1941 onwards at least 36 guns were sent to support Italian forces operating alongside the Germans on the Eastern Front, where they were organised into four eight-gun batteries, with four guns held in reserve. More served in North Africa. Their good all-round performance was noted by the Germans, so when Italy surrendered to the Western Allies in 1943 the German occupation forces were

The Cannone da 149/40 modello 35 showing the trail pickets

A blurred but lively shot of a Cannone da 149/40 modello 35 in action

quick to impound as many examples of the Cannone da 149/40 modello 35 as they could find to expand to their artillery holdings within Italy. The guns then became the 15cm K 408(i) and, in addition, the Ansaldo facility was ordered to manufacture more for issue to German forces operating in Italy. At least three were employed as coastal defence guns. By April 1944, 12 had been delivered, before the production line was closed down. There were plans to place these guns on turretless M 15/42 tank chassis to become self-propelled guns, but only one prototype was built.

Specification		
Calibre:	149.1mm	5.87in
Length of piece:	6,036mm	237.66in
Weight travelling (towed):	15,673kg	34,552lb
Weight in action:	11,340kg	25,004lb
Traverse:	60°	
Elevation, firing:	0 to +45°	
Muzzle velocity (max):	800m/s	2,625ft/sec
Max range:	23,700m	25,928yd
Shell weight:	46kg	101.4lb

Italy
Cannone da 152/45 M17

The Cannone da 152/45 M17 dated from about 1917, a time when the Italian army was in great need of long-range guns to counter the Austro-Hungarian army's well-equipped batteries. For what must have been originally regarded as a short-term measure the army took over stocks of reserve naval guns based on a Schneider design manufactured in Italy by OTO at La Spézia and meant for installation on Duilio class warships. Italian arsenals placed the barrels on land carriages, complete with a large shield, even though they were intended only for the static, long-range counter-battery role. Everything had to be carried on a convoy of carts and assembled on site, the gun barrel alone weighing 7,140kg (15,740lb). Installing the complete gun and carriage took a great deal of time and labour for, in the rush to get the naval guns into service, the mounting was

primitive and heavy, even if it was very steady during firing. For firing at high elevation angles, the norm along the mountainous Italian–Austrian border, where the guns were originally intended to be deployed, a deep pit had to be dug for the breech to recoil into. Hasty emplacements meant that the angle of traverse was limited to 10°. Further labour, including a widening of the recoil pit and installing a firing table or platform, could produce a more convenient traverse of 60° to cover a wider swathe of territory. Once the gun was in position the 46.7-calibre barrel could deliver a 47kg (103.6lb) projectile to a maximum 19,400m (21,223yd) range.

Well over 50 conversions had been completed by the time the war ended, and as late as September 1942 there were still 53 held available for use, plus five in reserve. By then most of them were still deployed along the

Good-quality illustrations of the Cannone da 152/45 M17 are hard to find ...

alpine border with Austria, usually held in depots ready to be carried to prepared firing sites, even though they were unlikely to be needed there. Other guns were re-allocated as coastal defence weapons guarding Italian naval bases. At least four types of projectile were available for this gun, two of them demonstrating their naval origins by being armour-piercing, but still with a useful role to play in the counter-battery role. Seven propellant charges were available, some of them again displaying their naval origins by requiring electrical rather than percussion ignition.

Specification		
Calibre:	152.4mm	6in
Length of piece:	7,138mm	281in
Weight travelling:	24,866kg	54,863lb
Weight in action:	16,672kg	36,762lb
Traverse:	10 or 60°	
Elevation, firing:	-5 to +45°	
Muzzle velocity (max):	830m/s	2,273ft/sec
Max range:	19,400m	21,223yd
Shell weight:	47kg	103.6lb

Italy
Obice da 149/19

After 1918 the Italian army's artillery park was filled with a wide variety of pieces from several countries (mainly from Austria-Hungary, France and Great Britain), most of them very ancient and well worn. By 1930 it had been decided that a measure of equipment uniformity had to be imposed to make training, logistics, and so on, more manageable. High on the list of requirements was a heavy field howitzer, so a series of experimental and trial models were ordered from OTO of La Spézia, and Ansaldo of Turin. The trials were directed by the Direzione Servizio Tecnico Armi e Munizione. The programme was conducted at a slow pace, so it was not until 1938 that a decision was made to manufacture an Obice da 149/19 modello 37, combining the best

features of the trial models. The manufacturing contract was split between OTO and Ansaldo, an initial and rather unrealistic order for 1,392 pieces being placed. A new family of ammunition was also ordered, although the Italian defence industry was in no position to manufacture such quantities without considerable plant, resources and machine tool investments, and that absorbed more time. By September 1942 only 147 examples had been delivered, although thereafter the production rate did increase somewhat, so by 1943 there were sufficient howitzers to equip 24 artillery battalions.

Only 16 examples of the initial modello 37 were made before production changed to the slightly modified modello 41 and then the modello 42. The

Under the camouflage finish is an Obice da 149/19

visible differences between all three models were small, although by increasing the chamber capacity and introducing a more powerful top charge the modello 42 had its maximum range increased by 1,005m (1,100yd). The maximum range of the modello 42 firing a 42.55kg (93.8lb) projectile was 15,300m (16,732yd). All three models had a 20-calibre barrel mounted on a sturdy, split-trail carriage without the usual shield.

The Italians regarded the Obice da 149/19 as one of the best weapons in its class then available. The Germans were sufficiently impressed to impound as many as they could for reissue to Wehrmacht divisions based in Italy. They knew the howitzer as the 15cm sFH 404(i) and maintained the type in production at OTO and Ansaldo until early 1945.

After 1945 any survivors of the war years were gathered in for further service with the post-war Italian army, some serving on until the mid-1950s before being replaced.

Specification		
Calibre:	149.1mm	5.87in
Length of piece:	3,034mm	119.5in
Weight travelling:	6,700kg	14,774lb
Weight in action:	5,500kg	12,125lb
Traverse:	50°	
Elevation, firing:	-3 to +60°	
Muzzle velocity (max):	597m/s	1,958ft/sec
Max range: modello 42	15,300m	16,732yd
Shell weight:	42.55kg	93.8lb

Italy
Mortaio da 210/8 DS

The Mortaio da 210/8 DS was another veteran from a previous era that somehow managed to be included in artillery returns dated after 1939. Its origins dated back to about 1900, when the piece (by definition a howitzer rather than a mortar, as stated in the designation) was intended for static use against heavy fortifications and similar targets. It was used during World War I, when the front lines along the border with Austria-Hungary were relatively stationary, but by 1940 there was little enough for

such elderly guns to do. Getting them in and out of action was a major undertaking, as all the gun parts had to be loaded onto trailers or transporters for even the slightest move. At a firing site a heavy timber firing platform (not included in transport weight) had to be erected on a levelled area before the howitzer was assembled. Once emplaced, after a great deal of labour, the howitzer then had a full 360° traverse.

Those remaining in 1940 were still located along Italy's northern alpine borders to cover passes and

The quaint-looking Mortaio da 210/8 DS, dating from about 1900

other likely invasion routes. There they remained throughout the war years, contributing little to military proceedings but maintained in a serviceable state in case they were needed. The barrel was only 9.7 calibres long overall, the length of bore being just 7.1 calibres. Most of the recoil forces were absorbed by the cradle on which the barrel rested. As the howitzer was fired, the cradle slid back along short inclined ramps. At the same time the entire upper carriage also slid back, on four wheels, to the rear along two inclined rails, being returned to the original position by a combination of gravity and return spring buffer housings.

The carriage was designed by Di Stefano, hence the 'DS' in the designation. From photographic evidence it seems that slight modifications were introduced to the carriage as production progressed, as no two examples looked quite the same in detail.

A five-charge propellant system propelled a 101.5kg (223.8lb) projectile to a maximum range of only 8,450m (9,224yd), adding to the high-explosive effects by the trajectory being almost vertical when the target was hit. By 1940 this lack of range, coupled with the mobility shortcomings, rendered the Mortaio da 210/8 DS almost worthless as an artillery asset, but such was the parlous state of the Italian artillery park, there was little to replace it. The antique therefore had to be retained.

Specification		
Calibre:	210mm	8.27in
Length of piece:	2,048mm	80.64in
Weight travelling:	5,790kg	12,765lb
Weight in action:	7,800kg	17,195lb
Traverse:	360°	
Elevation, firing:	-15 to +70°	
Muzzle velocity (max):	340m/s	1,115ft/sec
Max range:	8,450m	9,224yd
Shell weight:	101.5kg	223.8lb

Italy
Obice da 210/22 modello 35

Obice da 210/22 modello 35

The Obice da 210/22 modello 35 was another of the heavy-artillery designs selected for production to replace the Italian army's ageing artillery holdings during the 1930s. The design was drawn up by the army's own Direzione Servizio Tecnico Armi e Munizione department in 1938. Ansaldo were awarded the original production contract but OTO of La Spézia later had to become involved because the rate of production by Ansaldo was too slow to deliver sufficient numbers in the timescale originally scheduled. Even with OTO involved, production remained slow. The initial order, placed during 1940, was for 346 howitzers.

By September 1942 there were only 20 in service (15 of them serving alongside the Germans on the Eastern Front).

The modello 35 was a rather complicated piece of artillery, although rather prone to breakages when firing over prolonged periods. Despite this propensity, it was a good all-round, hard-hitting design that was well regarded at the time. The 23.8-calibre barrel could hurl a 101kg (222.7lb) projectile to 15,407m (16,855yd). There was also a heavier projectile weighing 133kg (293lb). The split-trail carriage had several unusual features. One was that, although the howitzer was fired from an under-carriage firing table that theoretically provided a full 360° traverse, the trail spades were held in position by pickets hammered through the end of the trail leg, and they had to be dug out again for any large traverse change. Although this approach was rather archaic by the early 1940s, it had the asset that the carriage was very stable when fired. The entire howitzer could be broken down into four tractor-drawn loads (plus another to carry accessories) for when operating in mountainous terrain, although two loads were more usual when the going allowed. For this the barrel was carried on a four-wheel transporter, while the carriage was towed on six wheels. Time in and out of action was about 30 minutes.

Despite the urgent need to get the modello 35 into Italian service in quantity, a batch was sold to Hungary prior to licence-production by MAVAG (the Hungarian State Railway workshops). By 1943 they were producing their own version with a strengthened carriage and some other modifications. The German army was another modello 35 user from 1943 until 1945. They knew the modello 35 as the 21cm H 520(i) and considered it good enough to maintain the type in production for Italy-based German artillery batteries after the Italian surrender.

Specification			
Calibre:	210mm	8.27in	
Length of piece:	5,000mm	196.9in	
Weight travelling:	24,030kg	52,976lb	
Weight in action:	15,885kg	35,026lb	
Traverse:	75°		
Elevation, firing:	0 to +70°		
Muzzle velocity (max):	560m/s	1,837ft/sec	
Max range:	15,407m	16,855yd	
Shell weight:	101 or 133kg	222.7 or 293lb	

An Obice da 210/22 modello 35 in service with the Hungarian army

Italy
Mortaio da 260/9 modello 16

A battery of Mortaio da 260/9 modello 16s on parade at their barracks; note the pre-prepared recoil pits

Exactly why the 260mm (10.23in) calibre was selected for the howitzer that became the Mortaio da 260/9 modello 16 is now uncertain, for it appears to have been the only artillery piece ever to be manufactured with this non-standard barrel dimension. It was built by Ansaldo, using design experience gained by the French Schneider concern, and first issued for service during 1916 (hence modello 16). It was deployed along the northern alpine borders with Austria-Hungary, where it was meant to destroy the numerous fortifications covering alpine passes through the mountains and other such invasion routes.

Compared to many other heavy howitzers of the time the modello 16 was advanced, as it could travel on its own wheels as a single load, being towed by a single large tractor, but once at a firing position it was back to the practices of a former era. For firing, the road wheels had to be removed, leaving the barrel and box trail to rest on a firing pedestal under the forward end of the carriage. If high angles of elevation were required a pit had to be dug under the breech area to cater for barrel recoil. A hasty installation resulted in a total on-carriage traverse of 6°, although further preparation (and digging) and the provision of a ground platform, could increase this to 60°. It appears that a shield to protect the howitzer mechanisms was optional. The projectile fired was heavy, 216kg (476.2lb), although the maximum possible range was limited to 8,100m (8,858yd). This projectile weight was more than enough to demand the use of a special handling and loading trolley to get the projectile into the breech. The effort involved meant that the practical rate of fire was usually about one round every ten minutes, although for short periods a trained crew could reduce the time between firings to one round every three minutes.

As the Mortaio da 260/9 modello 16 arrived rather late during the Great War, it was little used. Between the wars there was even less reason to loose off ammunition, other than a few rounds a year to keep the crews in a trained state and to impress visiting dignitaries. In 1940 the survivors (probably no more than a single battery) were still serviceable and hardly worn. They therefore had to be retained until some form of replacement arrived on the scene. It never did, because by 1940 the day of the heavy howitzer was almost over.

Specification		
Calibre:	260mm	10.23in
Length of piece:	2,703mm	106.4in
Weight travelling:	not found recorded	
Weight in action:	12,940kg	28,527lb
Traverse:	6 or 60°	
Elevation, firing:	+20 to +65°	
Muzzle velocity (max):	350m/s	1,148ft/sec
Max range:	8,100m	8,858yd
Shell weight:	216kg	476.2lb

Japan
150mm Gun Type 89

Although the Japanese army did own heavy artillery much of it was (at best) obsolescent by 1941. By that year virtually all the older and immobile equipments had been withdrawn from field service and relegated to coast- and beach-defence duties around mainland Japan. This left the field armies woefully short of up-to-date heavy artillery for counter-battery and interdiction tasks, the lack of which the overstretched Japanese industrial infrastructure was quite unable to rectify. There was only one viable Japanese weapon in the long-range artillery category, and that was the 150mm (5.87in) Gun Type 89. This gun was first produced in 1929 at the Osaka Arsenal, apparently with some design assistance lifted from Schneider of France.

The Schneider influence could be seen in the general appearance of the design, which was obviously influenced by the Schneider 155mm (6.1in) GPF, but in detail there was no comparison. In many ways the Type 89 was a much heavier and clumsy weapon. The high-velocity 30-calibre barrel could fire a heavy 45.9kg (101.12lb) projectile to a creditable 19,950m (21,800yd) range, but it did so at the expense of mobility. For towing by Model 92A tracked tractors the gun had to be broken down into two loads, barrel and carriage, so the time into action was slow, requiring at least two hours of hard labour before firing could commence. In the fighting that took place in China during the 1930s this lack of mobility apparently mattered little, so the Type 89 was considered satisfactory.

Once the combat tempo was increased to the rate encountered in the Malaya and Philippine campaigns the shortcomings of the Type 89 became more apparent. It was therefore gradually withdrawn from front-line service and relegated to coast- and beach-defence emplacements, where bulk and weight did not matter so much. US intelligence documents dated April 1945 make no mention of the Type 89.

During 1930 plans were made to place the ordnance of the Type 89 onto a more static carriage for siege work, but nothing appears to have come of that project. As all Japanese artillery was supposed to have an anti-tank function, armour-piercing high-explosive (APHE) projectiles were developed in addition to the more usual high-explosive and illuminating projectiles. One archaic touch was that a shrapnel projectile existed for use against massed infantry formations. It appears to have been little used other than sporadic employment in China.

Specification		
Calibre:	149.1mm	5.87in
Length of piece:	4,475mm	176in
Weight travelling:	not found recorded	
Weight in action:	10,409kg	22,928lb
Traverse:	40°	
Elevation, firing:	-5 to +43°	
Muzzle velocity (max):	686m/s	2,250ft/sec
Max range:	19,950m	21,800yd
Shell weight:	45.9kg	101.12lb

A side-view drawing of a 150mm (5.87in) Gun Type 89 showing the need for a recoil pit at high elevation angles

Japan
150mm Howitzer Type 4

The 150mm (5.87in) Howitzer Type 4 was designed at the Osaka Arsenal in 1915 and replaced the 150mm Howitzer Type 38, which had

been introduced in 1905 and was notable as the first howitzer produced at Osaka. It was intended that the Type 4 would overcome the range limitations of the

150mm Howitzer Type 4s on parade being towed by tracked tractors but still using limbers

150mm Howitzer Type 4 in action

Type 38, and it succeeded. By lengthening the barrel from 11 to 14.6 calibres and increasing the chamber volume the range, firing the same 35.9kg (79.16lb) projectile as the Type 38, was increased to 9,575m (10,464yd) – the Type 38 could manage only 5,900m/6,455yd. The Type 4 was the first Japanese artillery piece to have a hydro-pneumatic recoil system in place of the former springs.

Many of the main features of the Type 38 were carried over to the Type 4, including the remarkably light box carriage for the weight of projectile fired. The carriage was so light that it could not withstand towing over rough terrain without breaking, so for anything but the shortest moves the Type 4 barrel and rear trail section had to be removed and carried on a separate transporter trailer. Horse traction was originally used, replaced by the Type 98 or a similar tracked tractor during the 1930s. Whatever the towing method, the light construction still meant a

rate of progress of no more than 64km (40 miles) a day. Assembly and disassembly of the Type 4 was greatly facilitated by a system of removable rails and winches carried on the forward trail section. Thanks to this feature the time into action was reduced to about 10 minutes. Projectiles fired were mainly high-explosive or smoke/incendiary (filled with white phosphorus (WP)), although an illuminating projectile was available. The rate of fire for extended periods was from 30 to 40 rounds an hour. The fastest-possible firing rate by a well-trained crew was three to four rounds a minute, although for short periods only. Loading cannot have been eased by the sliding breech block, which opened vertically upwards, requiring considerable manual effort to operate over prolonged periods.

From 1936 onwards the Type 4 was supposed to be replaced by the 150mm Type 96 but the old howitzers were still around in 1945. As a result of the various campaigns in China, the Type 4 fell into Chinese Nationalist hands on a significant scale, so the Type 4 was employed by them until at least 1945.

Specification		
Calibre:	149.1mm	5.87in
Length of piece:	2,169mm	85.4in
Weight travelling:	4,340kg	9,568lb
Weight in action:	2,797kg	6,160lb
Traverse:	6°	
Elevation, firing:	-5 to +65°	
Muzzle velocity (max):	410m/s	1,345ft/sec
Max range:	9,575m	10,464yd
Shell weight:	35.9kg	79.16lb

Japan
150mm Howitzer Type 96

The 150mm (5.87in) Howitzer Type 96 was introduced in 1936 and manufactured in some numbers at the Osaka Arsenal. It was intended to replace the venerable Type 4 in service, although, thanks to the inadequacy of Japan's military production infrastructure, the best that could be achieved was to supplement the Type 4, the latter still remaining in service in 1945. In design terms the Type 96 was a completely new and state-of-the-art weapon that owed nothing to its predecessors. It took many of its carriage design features, scaled up, from the 105mm (4.14in) Type 92 field gun produced at Osaka during the early 1930s with assistance from Schneider of France. This meant the Type 96 had a split-trail carriage offering a useful traverse angle and, although heavier that the Type 4, the Type 96 could be towed at relatively high speeds as a single load.

The one feature that spoiled this appearance of modernity was the practice of securing the opened trail legs in position by hammering three trail spades down through a trail block at the end of each trail leg. Time into action was therefore about seven minutes. This feature was no doubt introduced due to experience of instability when firing early examples of the 105mm (4.14in) Gun Type 92 at extreme angles of traverse. One further time-absorbing shortcoming was the recoil pit that had to be dug under the breech area when fire missions involving elevation angles above 45° were conducted.

The rubber-tyred wheels remained wooden, even though the howitzer was meant to be towed by a Type 98 fully tracked tractor. When on tow the Type 96 utilised a leaf-spring suspension that was automatically disconnected as the trail legs were spread before firing. Another archaic feature was the carry-over of the Type 38 and Type 4 ammunition family to the Type 96, although the maximum range possible was increased to 10,365m (11,336yd), thanks mainly to extending the barrel length to 23.37 calibres. Once in service a new and lighter (30.8kg/67.9lb) streamlined projectile was introduced, enhancing the range still further to 11,860m (12,971yd). One feature of this ammunition was that breech obturation required the use of brass cartridge cases (containing up to five charges) at a time when raw materials were becoming increasingly scarce. The Type 96 screw was of the interrupted type in place of the sliding-block type favoured on earlier models.

Specification		
Calibre:	149.1mm	5.87in
Length of piece:	3,505mm	138in
Weight travelling:	4,924kg	10,846lb
Weight in action:	4,135kg	9,108lb
Traverse:	30°	
Elevation, firing:	-5 to +75°	
Muzzle velocity (max):	539m/s	1,768ft/sec
Max range:	10,365m	11,336yd
Shell weight:	35.9kg	79.16lb

Type 96 (1936) 150-mm Howitzer

An unusual overhead view of a 150mm Howitzer Type 96 taken from an intelligence manual

Sweden
Bofors 150mm m/31 Howitzer

A Bofors 150mm m/31 howitzer as delivered to Hungary

Although the Swedish 40mm (1.57in) Bofors air defence gun saw extensive combat service on all sides between 1939 and 1945 (due mainly to pre-1939 licence-production agreements) not many other Bofors defence products became involved in World War II. This, as always, was due to Sweden's carefully guarded state of neutrality, which extended (and still does) to not supplying defence products to any nation likely to use them in anger in the foreseeable future. As a result, potential markets in Europe were few up to 1939 (apart from equally neutral Switzerland and The Netherlands). Although Bofors continued to manufacture military equipment for domestic use at their Karlskoga facility between 1939 and 1945, little of their output was exported to participate in the world conflict. As always, there was one notable exception in our heavy artillery category. This was a commercial export model, the m/31 150mm (actually 149.3mm/5.88in) field howitzer, the ordnance partner to a smaller-calibre field gun, the 105mm (4.14in) m/31. Both pieces shared the same carriage and were so designed they could also be employed in the coastal defence role.

In common with other Bofors ordnance products, the 150mm m/31 was an advanced and sound design with few frills and an excellent all-round performance. The m/31 pairing found customers in South America, but the only pre-1939 European order came from Hungary, who purchased both the gun and the howitzer during the mid-1930s. To confound matters the Hungarian designation for both was 31 M. Exactly how many were purchased

remains unclear but one estimate puts the quantities for both at 36.

The 150mm m/31 was designed from the outset for mechanised traction so it could be towed by a Hungarian Pavesi tractor in one piece on rubber-tyred steel wheels. However, for long moves it was still recommended that the barrel and carriage should travel as separate loads. The robust split trail gave a good field of traverse at a time when such things were still novelties, while the 24-calibre barrel was considerably longer than many of its contemporaries. It could fire a 42kg high-explosive projectile to 14,700m (16,076yd), outranging many equivalents of the period. There was also a heavier projectile with a shorter range, as only one type of propellant charge was utilised.

From late 1941 onwards, the Hungarian army deployed their m/31 howitzers alongside German forces on the Eastern Front, where most of them were eventually lost.

Specification		
Calibre:	149.3mm	5.88in
Length of piece:	3,578mm	140.8in
Weight travelling:	6,600kg	14,550lb
Weight in action:	6,000kg	13,228lb
Traverse:	45°	
Elevation, firing:	-5 to +45°	
Muzzle velocity (max):	583 or	1,913 or
	530m/s	1,739ft/sec
Max range:	14,700m	16,076yd
Shell weight:	42 or	92.6 or
	47kg	103.6lb

Between the wars a few far-sighted Royal Artillery officers realised the need to re-equip their batteries following the experiences of the Great War. One of their requirements was for a new long-range gun to replace the 60-pounder (qv), with, as always, yet more range than before. Also, as ever, the funds to develop and acquire such a gun were non-existent. By the mid-1930s the need for a new gun was becoming urgent, although some limited funding was by then forthcoming. As the new gun was needed urgently it was decided that the new gun barrel and recoil mechanisms (a calibre of 4.5in (114.3mm) was selected) would be placed on readily available 60-pounder gun carriages. The carriages were modernised with pneumatic-tyred wheels and modern brakes for mechanical traction, plus a few other modifications to accommodate the new barrel. A total of 76 conversions were made, the first being ready for service in 1938.

The resultant 4.5in Gun Mark 1 on Carriage 60-pr Mark IV or IVP (the Mark IVP was by far the most numerous, as it was the version with the full mechanised traction kit) delivered all that had been asked for, but it was still regarded as a stopgap pending a purpose-designed gun-and-carriage combination. While the gun delivered the required range of 19,200m (21,000yd), the carriage proved cumbersome. Even so, the 4.5in Gun Mark 1 was among the better artillery pieces that the British Expeditionary Force took to France in 1940, and they acquitted themselves well enough during May and June 1940.

All 32 of the BEF Mark 1 guns were left behind after the Fall of France, most of them having been rendered useless by their crews and nearly all ammunition stocks having been either destroyed or fired off. Thus any serviceable guns that fell into German hands were of limited use to them – they knew the Mark 1 as the 11.4cm K 365(e). For a while the handful of ex-BEF survivors were stockpiled, only to be installed in the Atlantic Wall after 1941; few survived for long before being scrapped. Back in the UK most of the remaining Mark 1s were used for training purposes, while others were sent to North Africa, where they saw action during the early Western Desert battles. All of them had been withdrawn from service by 1943 and replaced by the 4.5in Gun Mark 2 (see following entry).

Specification		
Calibre:	114.3mm	4.5in
Length of piece:	4,881mm	192.2in
Weight travelling:	7,250kg	15,986lb
Weight in action:	5,730kg	12,635lb
Traverse:	7°	
Elevation, firing:	0 to +42°	
Muzzle velocity (max):	686m/s	2,250ft/sec
Max range:	19,200m	21,000yd
Shell weight:	24.95kg	55lb

United Kingdom
4.5-inch Gun Mark 2

The breech end of a 4.5in Gun Mark 2

As mentioned in the previous entry the 4.5in Gun Mark 1 was regarded only as a stopgap measure pending the availability of a better gun-and-carriage combination. In 1938 it was decided to develop a slightly revised version of the 4.5in (114.3mm) gun that could be accommodated on the carriage that was being designed for the 5.5in (139.7mm) gun-howitzer (qv). During August 1939 this project was approved but, even with the war having started, it took time to generate the necessary funding and production priorities. The establishment of a carriage production line also took time. Owing to early production and other difficulties the first carriages were not completed and approved for service until late 1940. Consequently, the first complete equipment was not delivered until mid-1941.

The complete official designation was BL, 4.5in Gun Mark 2 on Carriage 4.5in Gun Marks 1 and 2. There were few differences between the two carriage marks, which were both exactly the same as for the 5.5in gun-howitzer. In addition, both the gun and the gun-howitzer used the same breech mechanism. This commonality greatly reduced the time needed for training and other logistics. Distinctive features of the carriage were the two

equilibrator housings to balance the barrel at all angles of elevation, and the split trails providing a wide angle of traverse. Although regarded at one stage as being too light, the carriage proved sturdy and relatively easy to handle.

Churning up the dust with a towed 4.5in Gun Mark 2

Once in service the 4.5in Mark 2s were used for long-range counter-battery and interdiction fire missions within the Royal Artillery's Medium Regiments, but for this they were found to have one shortcoming, a lack of shell power. The high-explosive payload of the projectiles was too small, only 1.76kg (3.875lb) for a projectile weighing 24.95kg (55lb), to justify the expense and effort of delivering it. The 5.5in gun-howitzer using the same carriage could deliver a much heavier and more potent projectile to almost the same maximum range.

Gradually the 4.5in Gun Mark 2 fell from favour with increasing production emphasis (and gunner preference) being directed to the gun-howitzer, although 4.5in Mark 2 guns were still in the field when the war ended. After 1945 they were mostly relegated to training duties. During the late 1950s the last of them were withdrawn. It should be noted in the data below that the travelling weight refers to the weight when prepared for shipping.

Specification		
Calibre:	114.3mm	4.5in
Length of piece:	4,896mm	192.75in
Weight travelling:(shipping)	15,254kg	33,600lb
Weight in action:	5,847kg	12,880lb
Traverse:	60°	
Elevation, firing:	-5 to +45°	
Muzzle velocity (max):	686m/s	2,250ft/sec
Max range:	18,758m	20,500yd
Shell weight:	24.95kg	55lb

United Kingdom
60-pounder Gun

The origins of the 60-pounder Gun can be traced back to 1905, a time when British guns were designated according to their projectile weight.

Originally manufactured by the Elswick Ordnance Company, the gun was one of the mainstays of the British and Commonwealth medium batteries during the Great War. After 1918 Vickers-Armstrong reworked many of the numerous guns and carriages on hand in order to make them more amenable to towing by drawing the barrel back over the box trail so it formed a better balanced load between the main wheels and the limber wheels. (This was a reversion to the original design, abandoned during the war years to speed production.) Changes were also made to the breech and recoil mechanisms and the barrel was lengthened slightly. The result became the 60-pounder Gun Mark 2. A few Mark 3 carriages were manufactured as new. Later carriage modifications, by no means universally introduced, thanks to financial restrictions, involved the introduction of rubber- or pneumatic-tyred wheels suitable for towing by vehicles.

By 1939 the standard and preferred carriage was the 60-pounder Mark 4, with a hydro-pneumatic recoil system, although the piece was by then regarded as obsolete due to lack of range, poor handling, limited shell power and other considerations. Despite this, when the BEF went to France in 1939 they had to take 60-pounders with them as there was nothing else to hand. Although there were only 19 in France when the Germans invaded in May/June 1940, they were all left behind. As there was little ammunition left available to be fired, the Germans eventually scrapped what guns remained. The 60-pounders still in the UK were deployed for home defence, but were gradually relegated to training duties until they could be replaced. There were few left by 1944.

Batteries equipped with the 60-pounder took part in many of the early Western Desert battles, some of them in Australian hands. Other Commonwealth users were Canada and South Africa, the latter later introducing their own carriage modifications, including two relatively small wheels on a hinged beam on each side. The US army also had a few stockpiled 60-pounders, known to them as the 5in Gun M1918, left over from their adoption during the last year of the Great War. They never fielded them operationally, retaining them for training only. In 1940, 12 were sold to Brazil, where they served until the late 1960s.

Specification		
Calibre:	127mm	5in
Length of piece:	4,883mm	192.25in
Weight travelling:	6,423kg	14,148lb
Weight in action:	5,470kg	12,048lb
Traverse:	8°	
Elevation, firing:	-4.5 to +35°	
Muzzle velocity (max):	667m/s	2,176ft/sec
Max range:	13,816m	15,100yd
Shell weight:	27.24kg	60lb

United Kingdom
5.5-inch Gun

Although the 5.5in (139.7mm) Gun was officially described as a gun, it was more accurately described as a gun-howitzer, combining as it did the attributes of both types of artillery piece. It was originally proposed during the early 1930s as the replacement for the 6in (152.4mm) equipments then in service. Due to uncertainties and lack of funding, it was not until early 1939 that an operational requirement was issued for a suitable gun and carriage. Design and production difficulties intervened to delay the introduction of the eventual 5.5in Gun, called the Mark III to differentiate it from two naval guns with which it had nothing in common, until early 1942.

Thereafter it became the mainstay of British and Commonwealth medium artillery regiments and a true 'gunner's favourite'. Although the 5.5in Gun was bulky and heavy, it was reasonably easy to move and handle, and it fired a highly destructive projectile. The original high-explosive projectile weighed 45.4kg (100lb), resulting in a maximum range of 14,823m (16,200yd). Although good, this range was generally regarded as insufficient. That situation was rectified during 1943 by the introduction of a 36.32kg (80lb) projectile, together with an increased unitary top charge (all charges were bagged). The 36.32kg (80lb) projectile had the same external dimensions as its heavy counterpart but was made of a stronger grade of steel. The shell walls were therefore thinner, lighter and created better fragmentation on impact. Firing the lighter projectile resulted in a maximum possible range of 16,550m (18,100yd), almost the same as that for the 4.5in Gun Mark 2 (qv), which shared the same split-trail carriage (along with the same breech mechanism). With this increase in performance the 45.4kg (100lb) projectile fell by the wayside and was no longer used once existing stocks had been consumed. Several other ammunition natures were eventually developed including a smoke projectile.

The 5.5in Gun went on to provide steady,

A 5.5in Gun still serving on with the Royal Artillery in the late 1980s

A 5.5in Gun in action in North Africa

unremarkable and reliable service with several Commonwealth nations, including (among others) Australia, India, Pakistan, New Zealand and South Africa. With most of these nations the 5.5in gun-howitzer had a very extended service life, the last UK examples being used for firing projectiles to train forward observers until the late 1990s. South Africa was still developing special long-range, high-fragmentation projectiles for locally held 5.5s (known to them as the 140mm G2) during the late 1980s. This projectile had a maximum range of 21,000m (22,965yd).

Specification		
Calibre:	139.7mm	5.5in
Length of piece:	4,358.6mm	171.6in
Weight travelling:	6,423kg	14,148lb
Weight in action:	6,190kg	13,646lb
Traverse:	60°	
Elevation, firing:	-5 to +45°	
Muzzle velocity (max):	594m/s	1,950ft/sec
Max range:	16,550m	18,100yd
Shell weight:	36.32 or	80 or
	45.4kg	100lb

United Kingdom
6-inch Mark 19 Gun

The first 6in (152.4mm) guns went into British army service in 1915. The first results were regarded as highly unsatisfactory, so, as the 6in gun concept had been accepted as a useful weapon, a long and complex process of revised and modified marks ensued. The only solution was finally accepted as the design of an entirely new gun and a suitable carriage. This became the 6in Mark 19 Gun, with the 36.5-calibre barrel based around the ordnance of a generally similar coastal defence weapon. About 200 Mark 19s had been manufactured by the time the Great War ended, 100 of them for the US army in France. The Americans had disposed of their holdings by 1939, but somehow the British army still retained a few.

During the 1930s it was forecast that bomber aircraft would in future carry out most of the destructive tasks formerly carried out by heavy artillery. Heavy artillery holdings were therefore allowed to dwindle, so when the BEF went to France in 1939 there were only 12 Mark 19s available for them to take, plus one as a reserve. Those taken had at least been updated. The original carriage, basically the same as for the British 8in (203mm) Howitzer Mark 8 (qv) originally travelled on large, load-spreading, steel traction engine wheels. As these wheels were completely unsuitable for the mechanical traction used throughout the BEF, a limited number of carriages were provided with large pneumatic tyres, modern brakes, and a few other carriage modifications to allow the entire gun

to be towed in one load at a sedate pace. Only one type of high-explosive projectile was fired operationally, weighing approximately 45.4kg (100lb), the only alternative being a shrapnel shell for which few uses remained by 1940.

All the guns sent to France were either destroyed or fell into German hands during May and June 1940. As with other equipments, the Royal Artillery fired off or rendered useless as much ammunition as they could before they moved on, so very little remained for the Germans to utilise for their own purposes. Surviving trophy guns were therefore scrapped. Back in the UK the Mark 19 was retained for a while for home defence, training and morale-raising duties, most still on their traction engine wheels. Somehow a few saw action in North Africa. The last of them was declared obsolete in early 1944, their replacement being the 5.5in gun-howitzer (qv).

Specification		
Calibre:	152.4mm	6in
Length of piece:	5,568mm	219.22in
Weight travelling:	10,348kg	22,792lb
Weight in action:	10,348kg	22,792lb
Traverse:	8°	
Elevation, firing:	0 to +38°	
Muzzle velocity (max):	733m/s	2,405ft/sec
Max range:	17,156m	18,750yd
Shell weight:	45.4kg	100lb

A 6in Mark 19 Gun being used for training in 1941, still on traction-engine wheels

United Kingdom
QF, 4.5-inch, Howitzer Mark 2

The business end of the small but sturdy QF, 4.5in, Howitzer Mark 2

Field training with a QF, 4.5in, Howitzer Mark 2

For many armies, including the British, the QF, 4.5in, Howitzer Mark 2 was a light field howitzer, while to others it was the heaviest howitzer they fielded. It origins went back to 1909, when it was accepted as the field howitzer counterpart to the 18-pounder field gun. As such it served well and efficiently throughout the Great War, the only change from the original Mark 1 being that minor modifications were introduced to the sliding breech channel to prevent cracking following prolonged fire missions; the rifling was also simplified. Production was carried out at the Coventry Ordnance Works and Austin Motors, also at Coventry. After 1918 the search for a replacement began, but due to the large numbers still on hand the development of what became the 25-pounder field howitzer was prolonged. Before 1918, 4.5s had also been passed to numerous Commonwealth armies, while in 1917 400 were sent to Russia to assist the Tsarist army.

When the Great War ended the British army still had stocks of 984, with two million rounds still to be fired. After 1918 many more were handed on to numerous nations, including the new Baltic States.

During the 1930s it was accepted by the British that the 4.5 was obsolescent, but in the absence of anything better in the immediate future, the 4.5s were updated for mechanical traction by the installation of rubber-tyred wheels and suitable wheel bearings. With this conversion the British army went to France in 1939, only to lose almost

their entire holdings (96) to the Germans during 1940. The Germans did not adopt the 4.5, as hardly any ammunition was left in France to be captured. Those 4.5s left in the UK's post-1918 stockpiles were therefore dragged out again to be deployed for home defence and training, while overseas the 4.5 was again used in action in the Horn of Africa and during the early North African campaigning. Thereafter, sufficient 25-pounders were on hand to replace the ageing 4.5s.

By 1944 those survivors still used for training had been withdrawn. The type served on in Ireland until the late 1970s but again only as a training gun. For all its many users the 4.5 was a sound, sturdy howitzer that was light enough to be handled with relative ease. Its main drawback by 1940 was its lack of range, only 6,040m (6,600yd), and the light (but still useful) high-explosive projectile.

Specification		
Calibre:	114.3mm	4.5in
Length of piece:	1,778mm	70in
Weight travelling:	2,222kg	4,899lb
Weight in action:	1,494kg	3,293lb
Traverse:	6°	
Elevation, firing:	-5 to +45°	
Muzzle velocity (max):	305m/s	1,000ft/sec
Max range:	6,040m	6,600yd
Shell weight:	15.66kg	34.3lb

United Kingdom
6-inch 26cwt Howitzer Mark 1

A 6in 26cwt Howitzer Mark 1 as sent to France in 1939

The 6in 26cwt Howitzer Mark 1 entered British army service during 1915 as the replacement for the old 6in (152.4mm) 30cwt Howitzer. The term '26cwt' in the designation denoted the ordnance weight in hundredweights (2,912lb/1320kg) to differentiate the new howitzer from the old. For its

period the 6in 26cwt was an advanced design, being the first British mobile artillery piece to utilise a hydro-pneumatic recoil system. The overall design proved so sound it remained 'on the books' until late 1945, virtually unchanged from the original. A strong box-trail formed the basis of the carriage that accommodated the stubby 14.6-calibre ordnance. By the time of the Armistice about 4,000 had been produced, forming the backbone of the Royal Artillery's Medium Regiments.

Between the wars, batches of surplus guns were passed on to Belgium, The Netherlands, Italy and various Commonwealth nations such as Australia, but that still left several hundred either in service or stored around UK artillery establishments. By the late 1930s most of them had been provided with the usual pneumatic tyres and suitable brake modifications to enable them to be towed by mechanical tractors.

In 1939, 176 6in 26cwt howitzers were sent to France to support the BEF, plus another 45 to be held as combat reserves. They were all destroyed or changed hands as a result of the Fall of France in mid-1940, becoming an established part of the German armoury as the 15.2cm sFH 412(e), joined by yet more examples captured from Belgium, The Netherlands and, eventually, Italy. The booty was issued to several newly formed German divisions until something better came along. As the war progressed, most of the captured ammunition was either fired off or the barrels became worn, so by March 1944 only 21 remained. Back in the UK all

6in 26cwt howitzers that could be found were placed back into front-line service, initially for home defence and only later for the usual training roles. Numbers were sent to North Africa, where they served in Eritrea and the Western Desert until 1942, sometimes engaging the same model of howitzer in Italian hands (it was known by them as the Obice da 152/13). Others in the Far East served on until the war ended. Although the 6in 26cwt howitzer was supposed to be replaced by the 5.5in gun-howitzer, the latter remained only a supplement to their old predecessors until after the war ended.

Specification		
Calibre:	152.4mm	6in
Length of piece:	2,223mm	87.55in
Weight travelling:	4,471kg	9,849lb
Weight in action:	4,201kg	9,262lb
Traverse:	8°	
Elevation, firing:	0 to +45°	
Muzzle velocity (max):	429m/s	1,409ft/sec
Max range:	10,430m	11,400yd
Shell weight:	45.48kg	100.19lb

6in 26cwt Howitzer Mark 1s being used for training in Scotland, 1941

United Kingdom
7.2-inch Howitzer Marks 1 to 4

During the early 1930s the prospect of the bomber aircraft carrying out the role that heavy artillery had formerly fulfilled combined with a general lack of development funding to prevent almost entirely any new heavy artillery developments other than paper projects. One of

An early 7.2in Howitzer showing the recoil ramps

these paper exercises undertaken after about 1935 concerned two heavy weapons, a 6.85in (174mm) long-range gun and a 7.85in (200mm) howitzer on a common carriage. By 1939 both these projects had been dropped for several reasons, not the least being that there was a war on and something was desperately needed to replace the ancient heavy artillery then in service. By then the reliance on the bomber had been at least toned down as it was appreciated that artillery could keep firing when aircraft could not fly.

The immediate solution was a hasty improvisation. By taking old 8in (203mm) howitzer barrels and lining them down to 7.2in (182.9mm) a heavy 91.7kg (202lb) projectile could be fired to 15,464m (16,900yd), somewhere near what the gunners wanted. The relined barrels were placed on 8in howitzer box carriages updated by the introduction of large balloon tyres and suitable brakes to improve mobility. The conversions were rushed into service, where they soon displayed some alarming shortcomings. These were based around the fact that, when fired, the ordnance was too powerful for the recoil mechanisms and carriage to contain. On firing the top charges to obtain the maximum range, the howitzer bounced about and bucked alarmingly to the rear to the extent that the crew could not stand close without the risk of injury.

Due to the violent movement the howitzer had to be manhandled back to the firing position and relayed between each firing. Matters were only slightly improved by the provision of wedge-shaped ramps behind each wheel for the howitzer to travel up and down, but even those proved insufficient on occasion.

Such was the need for heavy artillery during 1941 to 1943 that the 7.2in howitzer had to be employed, but they were never popular, even though they provided excellent heavy fire support in North Africa and Italy. The four marks involved denoted the model of 8in howitzer barrel that had been relined, most of the barrels (Marks 2 to 4) having been produced in the USA during the Great War years. As soon as sufficient Mark 6 models became available (see following entry) the Marks 1 to 4 were withdrawn.

Specification		
Calibre:	182.9mm	7.2in
Length of piece:	4,343mm	171in
Weight travelling:	10,397kg	22,900lb
Weight in action:	10,397kg	22,900lb
Traverse:	8°	
Elevation, firing:	0 to +45°	
Muzzle velocity (max):	518m/s	1,700ft/sec
Max range:	15,464m	16,900yd
Shell weight:	91.7kg	202lb

United Kingdom
7.2-inch Howitzer Marks 5 and 6

By 1943 it had been accepted that the recoil-induced firing antics of the original 7.2in Marks 1 to 4 howitzer were such that it was decided to restrict firings to just the three less powerful propelling charges. The loss of the top (fourth) charge meant that range was reduced accordingly, something the gunners understandably did not wish

for, so development work on a more suitable carriage began. That work ceased once the first assignments of the M1 carriage for US 155mm (6.1in) guns and 8in (203mm) howitzers began to arrive in the UK during 1943. It was realised that with some appropriate carriage modifications, the 7.2in (182.9mm) barrel could be placed on the M1 split-trail carriage, rendering further home-generated carriage development pointless.

Trials to determine if this potential could be realised soon demonstrated that it was, the barrel and M1 carriage combination becoming the 7.2in Howitzer Mark 5. The prospect then arose that instead of placing an old barrel on a new carriage, an entirely new and longer barrel would produce even better results. A 34.4-calibre 7.2in barrel was therefore developed and produced with commendable speed and substituted for the 23.7-calibre barrel of the Mark 5, and the far more powerful Mark 6 was born. In the process the Mark 5, although accepted for service, was discarded, so that model was never issued for front-line service. From early 1944 onwards the Mark 6 howitzer gradually replaced the earlier marks, which were then retired, with few regrets from the gunners who had to use them.

The Mark 6 barrel and M1 carriage combination proved to be excellent in service, being stable, accurate and capable of remaining in action for prolonged periods; all factors that were used to the full from the D-Day landings until the end in May 1945. The Mark 6 barrel was also capable of accepting an extra (fifth) top charge, providing the power to fire the same 91.7kg (202lb) high-explosive projectile as before to 17,995m (19,667yd). In addition the extra elevation and traverse angles made available by the M1 carriage provided the howitzer with increased tactical flexibility.

After 1945 the 7.2in Mark 6 served on with the Royal Artillery's Heavy Regiments until the late 1960s. Most of the howitzers and their remaining ammunition were then sold to India where, in 2003, the Mark 6 is still retained to demolish potential urban warfare targets.

Specification		
Calibre:	182.9mm	7.2in
Length of piece:	6,300mm	248in
Weight travelling:	13,220kg	29,120lb
Weight in action:	13,220kg	29,120lb
Traverse:	60°	
Elevation, firing:	-2 to +65°	
Muzzle velocity (max):	587m/s	1,925ft/sec
Max range:	17,995m	19,667yd
Shell weight:	91.7kg	202lb

Victory in 1945, with 7.2in Howitzer Mark 5 or 6s on parade

United Kingdom
8-inch Howitzer Mark 8

The 8in (203mm) heavy howitzer that would become the Howitzer Mark 8 had its origins in 1916 when a Mark 7 was introduced into British army service. Over the inter-war years the early Mark 7 pieces were gradually updated to Mark 8 standard, so when World War II began in September 1939 only the Mark 8 remained. Most of the relatively small number in service by then had undergone the usual updating procedure of being provided with large balloon-type tyres to render them suitable for mechanical traction. However, a few still retained the original wide traction engine wheels fitted to the original Great War examples. The carriage was the same as that employed for the 6in (152.4mm) Gun Mark 19 (qv).

By 1939 the Mark 8 was regarded as obsolete, being capable of firing a 90.8kg (200lb) high-explosive projectile to 11,346m (12,400yd) using a six-increment propelling charge system. But in 1939 there was nothing else available, thanks mainly to a lack of inter-war funding to develop a replacement, so when the BEF went to France they took just 12 Mark 19s, plus one reserve piece. All of them were lost during the Fall of France in mid-1940 – the Germans appear to have scrapped them, as there is no record of any being retained.

Back in the UK the 8in Mark 8 once again became an important artillery asset for a while, before the carriages and barrels were 'cannibalised'

as the basis for the early 7.2in (182.9mm) howitzers, the old barrels being relined to the new calibre.

By late 1943 the 8in Mark 8 had faded from the scene. There was one further 8in howitzer, the US 8in Howitzer M1917. In 1916 orders had been placed in the USA by the British Ministry of War to boost the numbers to be sent to the Fronts, and in late 1917 the type was also type-classified for US army service. In 1941 there were still about 200 scattered around at various US bases. They were not employed operationally. Instead they added to the war effort by having their old barrels removed to be sent to the UK for relining to 7.2in and becoming the 7.2in Howitzer Marks 2 to 4. The basic 8in 'British' barrels were also used as the starting point for a series of US developments which have ensured the 8in howitzer remains a viable weapon to this day.

Specification		
Calibre:	203mm	8in
Length of piece:	3,767mm	148.3in
Weight travelling:	9,101kg	20,048lb
Weight in action:	9,101kg	20,048lb
Traverse:	8°	
Elevation, firing:	0 to +45°	
Muzzle velocity (max):	457m/s	1,500ft/sec
Max range:	11,346m	12,400yd
Shell weight:	90.8kg	200lb

Loading an 8in Howitzer Mark 8

United Kingdom
9.2-inch Howitzer Mark 2

The original 9.2in (234mm) howitzer appeared in 1910 as the Mark 1. The Mark 2 appeared during 1916, having been developed to meet requests for extra range. The former 14.5-calibre barrel was therefore replaced by the Mark 2's 18.5-calibre barrel, which gave the howitzer a range of 12,742m (13,935yd) firing a 131.5kg (290lb) high-explosive projectile, and the recoil mechanism was strengthened accordingly.

The design of the Mark 2 carriage was considered quite advanced for the period, but remained centred around the classic siege howitzer designs of the early 1900s in that the howitzer was set on a firing table onto which the carriage had to be placed for firing. Getting the howitzer into action took at least half a day. That was suitable enough for static trench warfare but of very little use during mechanised warfare. For moves the howitzer had to be carried in three main loads (plus three more for accessories and ammunition). One of the main loads was the howitzer's firing platform and the walls and bottom of a prefabricated steel earth box placed in front of the installed firing platform and filled with earth to add stability during firing.

By 1940 there was no real combat role for the 9.2in Mark 2 to play, but 24 (plus three reserves) were sent to France in 1940 to bulk out the BEF's heavy artillery park. In the event their immobility dictated they had little part to play when the Germans invaded France and all the howitzers

were lost. The Germans had scrapped them by 1943, despite bestowing the designation of 23.4cm H 546/2 (e) upon their trophies. As almost all available 9.2in howitzer ammunition had been sent to France there was very little left in the UK and there were no longer any facilities for manufacturing any.

The few 9.2in howitzers remaining in the UK after mid-1940 therefore had limited prospects, even for training, so they were installed, along with a few rounds for each, at likely invasion points and left there until they could be withdrawn and scrapped, after 1942. In 1940 there were plans to develop a new 9.2in howitzer that could be towed as one load by a heavy tractor. A maximum range of 14,630m (16,000yd) with a projectile weighing 143kg (315lb) was specified. The project got as far as the prototype hardware stage before the entire project was terminated in late 1942.

Specification		
Calibre:	234mm	9.2in
Length of piece:	4,331mm	170.51in
Weight travelling:	not found recorded	
Weight in action:	16,443kg	36,228lb
Traverse:	60°	
Elevation, firing:	+15 to +50°	
Muzzle velocity (max):	488m/s	1,600ft/sec
Max range:	12,742m	13,935yd
Shell weight:	131.5kg	290lb

The main role for the 9.2in Howitzer Mark 2 after 1940 – training

Illustration of a 9.2in Howitzer Mark 2 from a German recognition manual

United Kingdom
12-inch Howitzer

The British 12in (305mm) howitzer has only a tenuous reason for being in this summary, for as early 1918 it was already being regarded as the cumbersome anachronism it undoubtedly was. The first example appeared during 1917. Vickers were responsible for the design, simply scaling up the existing 9.2in (234mm) howitzer (see previous entry). Also scaled up from the 9.2in howitzer was the 12in howitzer's immobility. Any move required a considerable team of labourers as well as gunners, for the piece had to move in no less than six loads.

They were barrel, cradle, carriage, two positioning beams, an earth box, plus beams to form the main firing platform, all towed by steam engines or tracked tractors. The total weight of all these loads and their special transporters cannot be found recorded, but it was heavy. The reason for the earth box became apparent when it was secured to the front of the assembled firing platform. It had to be filled with tons of earth to act as a recoil anchor and had to be emptied again before the next move. Once emplaced, the 12in Howitzer was a powerful weapon, firing a 340.2kg (750lb) high-explosive projectile. This projectile was heavy enough to warrant a power rammer during loading. Using an eleven-part propelling charge system the maximum range was 13,120m (14,350yd).

How many 12in howitzers were made is not known but it cannot have been many. Some time after 1918 a small number were sent to Russia to assist the White Russians during the Russian civil war. Mention of these howitzers appeared in intelligence summaries as late as 1941 but it is doubtful that any had survived until then. The only connection of the 12in howitzer with World War II came in 1939 when just four were sent to support the British Expeditionary Force in France, together with all available ammunition. By then the original six loads were still necessary, even though heavy Scammell tractors had been introduced, so the cumbersome factor remained. When the Germans invaded France in May 1940 there was little that the 12in howitzers could contribute to proceedings. At some stage they were rendered unserviceable by their crews, leaving the wreckage to be scrapped by the Germans. The very few 12in howitzers still in the UK had virtually no ammunition, so they were withdrawn, other than as morale-raising items to impress the public. They were finally declared obsolete in 1945.

Specification		
Calibre:	305mm	12in
Length of piece:	5,647.7mm	222.35in
Weight travelling:	not found recorded	
Weight in action:	38,100kg	84,000lb
Traverse:	60°	
Elevation, firing:	+20 to +65°	
Muzzle velocity:	447m/s	1,468ft/sec
Max range:	13,120m	14,350yd
Shell weight:	340.2kg	750lb

USA
4.5-inch Gun M1

One of the recommendations of the Westervelt Board, a committee established in 1919 to determine what future artillery pieces would be required by the US army, was for a 4.7in (119.4mm) gun which would share the same carriage as a proposed 155mm (6.1in) howitzer. Some development work was carried out, resulting in the Gun M1922E. As with so many US artillery projects of that era, funds were short and the entire project was shelved during 1928. By 1939 the urgency for such a gun was becoming more pressing, so the old 1928 drawings were dusted off and the resultant 4.7in gun was installed on the same split-trail carriage as the 155mm Howitzer M1 then being developed in parallel. Prototypes were manufactured before a change of emphasis intervened. It was decided that the calibre should be altered to 4.5in (114.3mm) to introduce some measure of logistic and ballistic standardisation between British and US batteries, even though at that time the USA had not yet entered World War II. In the event the British-pattern ammunition was standardised as the shell, HE 4.5in M65, the bulk of the US Army's ammunition being manufactured in Canada.

The overall result was the 4.5in Gun M1 on Carriage M1 or M1A1. The only difference between the two carriages was that the M1 had air brakes, while those for the M1A1 were electrically controlled. The 42-calibre barrel of the Gun M1 had a good range, being able to reach out to 19,137m (21,125yd) with a supercharge increment added to

the usual two-part charge, but there was a drawback. As it fired the same projectile as the British 4.5in gun it suffered from the same shortcoming. The gun's M65 projectile (no other type was introduced) suffered from the same lack of explosive payload as its British counterpart, so the on-target effect was insufficient for all the efforts involved. As the gun was in production it was decided to keep manufacturing them but at a lower priority than had originally been planned.

Only a relative few saw action in Europe, the bulk of the output being retained in the USA for training purposes. When the war ended just 426 had been produced, along with 1,969,000 projectiles. Production then ceased and the type was withdrawn from service. A project to mount the Gun M1 on a self-propelled carriage based around the M3 light tank chassis was cancelled during mid-1944.

Specification		
Calibre:	114.3mm	4.5in
Length of piece:	4,919.7mm	193.7in
Weight travelling:	5,654kg	12,445lb
Weight in action:	5,654kg	12,445lb
Traverse:	53°	
Elevation, firing:	0 to +60°	
Muzzle velocity (max):	694m/s	2,275ft/sec
Max range:	19,137m	21,125yd
Shell weight:	24.97kg	55lb

Destined to be manufactured in limited quantities only, the 4.5in Gun M1

USA
155mm Gun M1917A1 and M1918A1

When the first American troops arrived in France in 1917 they were highly impressed by the 155mm (6.1in) GPF gun (qv) loaned to them

by the French. They decided to adopt it as one of their standard equipments, placing orders in France and sending drawings back to the USA for

155mm Gun M1917A1 or M1918A1 gun crews undergoing training

A 155mm Gun M1917A1 ready for towing

production undertaken at Watervliedt Arsenal and a specially built facility at Bridgeport, Connecticut. Guns manufactured in France were designated M1917, while US guns became the M1918. The two models were virtually identical to allow components to be exchanged between the two. By the end of 1918, 354 M1918s had been manufactured in the USA.

Between the wars both models were provided with roller-type wheel bearings to assist towing by mechanised tractors, raising both models to the 'A1' standard. From 1937 two patterns of 'high-speed' carriage with pneumatic wheels and air brakes were introduced; they were the Carriage M2 and M3 for the M1917 and M1918 respectively. By June 1940, the US Army had a holding of 973 M1917A1 and M1918A1 guns. Most of them were then held in depots, although numbers were deployed as mobile coastal defence guns around mainland USA and Pacific Island bases. The coastal defence guns were held at central points ready to be rushed to the sector where and when they were needed. At the chosen site they were lifted onto pre-prepared 'Panama Mounts', concrete emplacements with a fixed steel racer ring. Once on the Panama Mount racer ring the gun could be turned through a full 360° traverse.

By 1940 the M1917A1 and M1918A1 were regarded as obsolescent, although, as sufficient replacements were not yet available (see following entry), the type was retained in service. Some saw active service in the Philippines in 1941/42 while other guns were deployed to Sicily and were used in action during the early stages of the Italian campaign. By 1943 remaining stocks had been passed to Allied nations as diverse as Australia, Brazil and the Free French. In the USA about 100 barrels were removed from their towed carriages and adapted for the Gun Motor Carriage M12, based on a much-modified Medium Tank M3 (Lee) chassis. About 100 M12s were produced, only for most to be stockpiled until a use could be found for them. That use arrived after June 1944, when 74 were sent to Europe. They remained active until the war ended, providing sterling service wherever they appeared.

Specification		
Calibre:	155mm	6.1in
Length of piece:	5,887mm	231.8in
Weight travelling:	14,884kg	32,813lb
Weight in action:	11,750kg	25,905lb
Traverse:	60°	
Elevation, firing:	0 to +35°	
Muzzle velocity (max):	735m/s	2,410ft/sec
Max range:	18,380m	20,100yd
Shell weight:	43kg	94.8lb

USA
155mm Gun M1A1

Attempts to improve on the 155mm (6.1in) M1917/M1918 gun (see previous entry) began as early as 1920. The project was soon shelved for the usual reason, lack of funding, only to resume at a slow pace during the early 1930s – it was planned that the carriage could also accommodate an 8in (203mm) howitzer. By 1938 the end result had been type-classified as the 155mm Gun M1 on Carriage M1; 65 had been manufactured by the end of 1941.

The M1 gun did not last long before changes to breech manufacture resulted in the M1A1. One feature of the breech mechanism was that the original Schneider breech of the M1917/M1918 was changed to an interrupted-screw type with a spring-assisted closing system for use at high angles of elevation. The split-trail M1 carriage was to prove one of the piece's best and most durable features. It was of the high-speed towing type designed for mechanical traction, and its split trails provided a sturdy and steady platform when firing. For towing, the trails were raised onto a two-wheel limber and travelled on four tyres on each side; all the tyres were pneumatic. (It was this carriage that was later adapted by the British for their 7.2in (183mm) Howitzer Mark 6 (qv)). For travelling, the 45-calibre barrel was disconnected from the recoil mechanism and pulled back over the joined trails. The 45-calibre barrel could fire the same 43kg (94.8lb) M101 high-

155mm Gun M1A1s in action on the Rhine, 1945

A 155mm Gun M1A1 on tow behind an M1 tracked tractor

explosive projectile as for the M1917/M1918 to 23,221m (25,395yd). On occasion, the Gun M1 was also employed for coastal defence, making use of the prefabricated steel T6E1 'Kelly Mount', a portable variant of the earlier fixed Panama Mount. The T6E1 could be erected wherever needed and then dismantled and carried away for further use elsewhere.

Widely known as the 'Long Tom', the 155mm Gun M1A1 went on to become one of the most widely used and successful of all Allied long-range guns. The US Army were far from being the only users, as many were handed to Allied nations (including the British), especially during the post-war years. A self-propelled version, the Gun Motor Carriage M40, was developed during the war years,

but none entered service before the war ended. With all its many owners the Gun M1 had a very long and distinguished service career but it gradually faded away and is no longer in service anywhere.

Specification		
Calibre:	155mm	6.1in
Length of piece:	7,336mm	290in
Weight travelling:	13,880kg	30,423lb
Weight in action:	12,600kg	27,777lb
Traverse:	60°	
Elevation, firing:	-1.5 to +63°	
Muzzle velocity (max):	853m/s	2,800ft/sec
Max range:	23,221m	25,395yd
Shell weight:	43kg	94.8lb

USA
8-inch Gun M1

As with so much American World War II artillery, the 8in Gun M1 had its origins in the early 1920s, when consideration was given to placing an 8in (203mm) railway gun on a roadworthy towed mounting. Little work was done before the project was shelved in 1924, only for it to recommence in 1939, the intention being to provide a counterpart to a 240mm (9.49in) howitzer also under consideration at that time; both would share the same carriage. The programme was plagued with troubles. One was that

the internal ballistics of the barrel proved difficult to master, even though it was of completely conventional design and 50 calibres long. The charges were large and heavy, causing excessive barrel erosion and poor accuracy. Numerous trial barrels were produced and fired but few improvements were made. Then there was the sheer scale and mass of the gun-and-carriage combination. Overall dimensions and weights were such that the gun had to be towed in two loads on special 87 transport wagons, as with many other large artillery pieces, but assembly and disassembly had to be carried out by using a truck-mounted 20-ton crane that accompanied each gun. Normal tractors were not powerful enough to tow the loads at the specified road speed of 25mph (40km/h), so turretless M3 medium tank chassis had to be employed and the required speed was rarely achieved. In addition to all this a recoil pit had to be excavated under the breech when high elevation angles were required.

It was January 1944 before the gun and carriage were type-classified, and thereafter production was slow, resource consuming and expensive. Only 109 were manufactured and only a handful of them were ever used in action, although the British Army did receive a few.

Once in Europe the 8in gun proved very useful for demolishing large targets at long ranges. It fired a 108.8kg (240lb) projectile to 32,585m (35,635yd) at a steady rate of fire of one round every one to two minutes. The range was less than had been planned, as the original propellant charges had to be reduced in an attempt to overcome the barrel wear problem. All the efforts put into the 8in Gun M1 were hardly worth the result, as it was simply too ponderous for the type of warfare prevalent by 1944/45. At one stage a barrel was placed onto the tracked 8in Gun Motor Carriage T93, but only one was produced.

Specification		
Calibre:	203mm	8in
Length of piece:	10,401mm	409.5in
Weight travelling:	47,047kg	103,720lb
Weight in action:	31,434kg	69,300lb
Traverse:	30°	
Elevation, firing:	+10 to +50°	
Muzzle velocity (max):	866m/s	2,840ft/sec
Max range:	32,585m	35,635yd
Shell weight:	108.8kg	240lb

The figure standing on the carriage provides an indication of the scale of the 8in Gun M1

USA
155mm Howitzer M1917 and M1918

In many ways the development histories of the 155mm (6.1in) M1917 and M1918 howitzers ran in parallel with that of the 155mm Gun M1917 and M1918 (qv). Both were selected as standard equipments for the US Army soon after they arrived in France in 1917, with Schneider producing the first model, the M1917, in France by continuing the 155mm C 17 S (qv) production line until the war ended. At least four M1917 sub-marks existed, as the carriages were gradually altered to suit US Army requirements. As with the guns, C 17 S drawings were sent to the USA for production to start there, and US-produced guns became the M1918. There were some differences between the French M1917 and US M1918, the main visible difference being that the shield for the M1917 was curved, while that on the M1918 was straight, to simplify production.

By December 1918, 1,695 M1918s had been manufactured in the USA. Between the wars many were stockpiled, still unused. Some modernisation was carried out when funds became available from 1937 onwards, and an 'All-American' ammunition suite of projectiles, fuzes and propellant charges was developed and introduced. Out of the 2,971 M1917/M1918 examples still 'on the books' in June 1940, 599 had been 'high-speeded'. This involved the provision of pneumatic-tyred wheels, roller bearings and brakes to permit the howitzer and carriage to be towed by a truck, to which it was connected by a drawbar. Not all US-held examples were so modified.

Service-manual illustration of a 155mm Howitzer M1917 as delivered to the British army in 1940

By 1940 the M1917 and M1918 howitzers were scheduled for replacement, but the type soldiered on until 1945, although not in American hands (other than for training purposes). Once the early war years were over large numbers of M1917 and M1918 howitzers were handed over to many Allied nations with limited artillery assets. The British and South Africans used many in North Africa and during the early stages of the Sicilian and Italian campaigns.

Australia was another recipient as, no doubt to their chagrin, were the Free French. After US deployments in the Philippines in late 1941 and early 1942, examples of both models went on to further their Far East careers by serving with the Chinese fighting the Japanese. Many more were handed over to several South American states – four that were passed to Brazil were still being maintained in an operational state during the mid-1960s.

Specification		
Calibre:	155mm	6.1in
Length of piece:	2,332mm	91.8in
Weight travelling:	4,321kg	9,518lb
Weight in action:	3,715kg	8,184lb
Traverse:	6°	
Elevation, firing:	0 to +42°	
Muzzle velocity (max):	451m/s	1,478ft/sec
Max range:	11,250m	12,295yd
Shell weight:	42.8kg	94.27lb

The straight shield denotes this is a 155mm Howitzer M1918

By 1939 the US ordnance authorities were finally given funding to design a new 155mm (6.1in) howitzer to replace the M1917 and M1918, with their limited-traverse and mobility shortcomings. Much of the design work on the new howitzer was carried out at the Rock Island Arsenal. So sound was the final product that it remains in widespread service all around the world in the 21st century and shows no signs of fading away from many armies.

The new howitzer, the 155mm Howitzer M1, shared the same carriage as the 4.5in (114.3mm) Gun M1 (qv), devised from 1934 onwards, but was manufactured in far greater numbers. By 1945, 4,035 Howitzer M1s had been manufactured – the final production post-war total was just over 6,000.

These totals marked the high degree of reliance placed on the Howitzer M1, for it proved to be rugged, accurate and highly effective, serving wherever the US Army ventured. A measure of its sound but conventional design was that the last howitzer manufactured was much like the first, although an M1A1 model used stronger steels in its construction. A few carriage modifications were introduced, none of them drastic. The 20-calibre barrel could reach 14,640m (16,000yd) firing the 43.14kg (95lb) M107 high-explosive shell, which remains a widely manufactured and deployed munitions mainstay for many armies to this day.

Ammunition from the earlier howitzer series was not suitable for the new barrel, so a new suite was developed from the earlier types. The resultant projectiles and propelling charges remain almost unchanged for numerous other artillery pieces to this day. Firing involved lowering a firing table from under the carriage so the resultant split trail-leg-and-table combination kept the howitzer steady once in action. A self-propelled carriage, the 155mm Howitzer Motor Carriage M41, based on the chassis of the M24 light tank chassis and widely known as the Gorilla, was devised rather late in the war, so the bulk of them, about 100 or so, served on for many years after 1945.

After 1945 the M1 was widely copied direct, while another post-war development is still in progress. The basic carriage proved so sound that, with a little strengthening in some critical areas, it has been converted to accommodate powerful 39-calibre barrels firing enhanced range ammunition. A post-war re-designation system changed the original Howitzer M1 title to Howitzer M114 – no changes were made to the howitzer itself.

Specification		
Calibre:	155mm	6.1in
Length of piece:	3,810mm	150in
Weight travelling:	12,786kg	5,800lb
Weight in action:	12,698kg	5,760lb
Traverse:	53°	
Elevation, firing:	-2 to +63°	
Muzzle velocity (max):	564m/s	1,850ft/sec
Max range:	14,640m	16,000yd
Shell weight:	43.14kg	95lb

RA PD 45923

USA
8-inch Howitzer M1

The 1919 Westervelt Board, charged with determining the US army's future artillery requirements, proposed that an 8in (203mm) howitzer better than the British-derived models then in service should be introduced. Using the British 8in howitzer design as a basis, some development work was carried out before the money ran out in 1921. The project was revived in 1927, although it was 1929 before hardware appeared, and that project also lapsed. By 1940, and with the requirement becoming urgent, it was decided to place a 25-calibre 8in barrel on the same split-trail carriage design as the 155mm (6.1in) Gun M1 (Long Tom) although, once installed, the gun and howitzer could not be interchanged on the same carriage. The barrels of the gun and howitzer shared the same breech mechanism.

The howitzer became the 8in Howitzer M1 on Carriage M1, with production commencing during 1942. By 1945, 1,006 examples had been manufactured, late-production barrels (the M2) having a revised method of securing the breech mechanism to the barrel. As with its gun counterpart, the Howitzer M1 proved to be a steady and sturdy artillery weapon capable of delivering accurate fire for prolonged periods. The usual rate of fire during sustained fire missions was one round every two minutes. For 'rapid' fire this could be increased to one round a minute. Towing required an M4 high-speed tracked tractor or a 7.5-ton 6 x 6 truck.

Although the Howitzer M1 had less range than its gun counterpart (16,937m (18,510yd)) it fired a powerful 90.8kg (200lb) – almost twice as heavy as the projectile for the gun – high-explosive projectile, so it was often more favoured as an all-round artillery piece once in the field. The high-explosive projectile, the M106, remains in widespread service to this day, still being fired from towed and self-propelled howitzers all around the world, although some have been phased out in favour of artillery rocket systems.

A post-war re-designation system changed the original towed Howitzer M1 title to Howitzer M115 – no alterations were made to the howitzer itself. A self-propelled carriage, the 8in Howitzer Motor Carriage M43, was devised but the first examples did not enter US Army service until 1946. The M43 was the first of a series of self-propelled equipments that continue to fire the same 8in/203mm ammunition as the Howitzer M1, but from longer barrels providing much more range.

Specification		
Calibre:	203mm	8in
Length of piece:	5,323mm	209.6in
Weight travelling:	14,515kg	32,005lb
Weight in action:	13,471kg	29,703lb
Traverse:	60°	
Elevation, firing:	-2 to +64°	
Muzzle velocity (max):	595m/s	1,950ft/sec
Max range:	16,937m	18,510yd
Shell weight:	90.8kg	200lb

The power of the 8in Howitzer M1 is well illustrated in this action shot

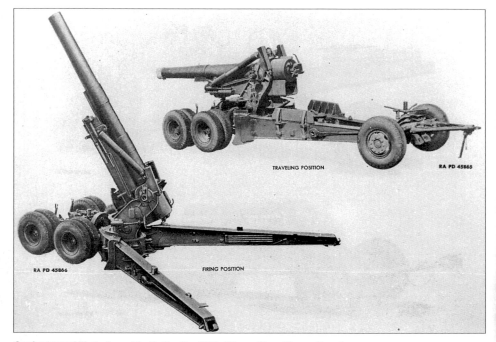

TRAVELING POSITION   RA PD 45865

RA PD 45866   FIRING POSITION

Service manual illustrations of the 8in Howitzer M1 in firing and travelling configurations

USA
240mm Howitzer M1

The US Army's first 240mm (9.45in) heavy howitzer was the M1918, a Schneider design ordered in 1918 but not ready for service until the mid-1920s. This was due to several reasons, one of which was the difficulty in manufacturing the complicated design and another that something went wrong with the internal ballistics of the barrel and it took years of development work to eradicate the problems. Even after that the M1918 was still not deemed a successful weapon, so those eventually delivered took no part in Second World War proceedings other than for training purposes. By 1939 it was considered that the M1918 was quite unsuitable for modern warfare, so another design had to be devised, leading to the 240mm Howitzer M1 on Carriage M1.

This howitzer shared the same massive, strut-braced, split-trail carriage as the 8in Gun M1 (qv). It thus suffered from the same bulk and mass problems, together with the two-part travelling configuration (barrel and carriage) and the need for a truck-mounted crane to assemble the complete

equipment once at a firing site. In addition, a large recoil pit had to be dug under the breech, as with the gun. Emplacement, using hand winches and digging the pit manually, could take well over eight hours of hard labour, but could be reduced to about two hours if a 20-ton crane truck was available, especially if it had digger buckets for excavating the recoil pit. However, these shortcomings were at least partially overcome by the howitzer proving itself to be an excellent and accurate weapon capable of neutralising stout structures and other well-protected targets at ranges up to 23,065m (25,225yd). The standard M114 high-explosive projectile (the only type fired) weighed 163.3kg (360lb) and was specifically developed for the Howitzer M1, having nothing to do with the ammunition suite for the earlier M1918.

By 1945 these M114 projectiles were being provided with proximity fuzes, vastly improving their overhead burst effects. The 240mm Howitzer M1 was employed by both the US and British armies from mid-1943 onwards and provided sterling service in Europe, especially during the Italian campaign. An attempt to place the howitzer on an M26 medium tank chassis resulted in the T92, widely known as the King Kong. Only five were manufactured before the war ended and the project was terminated. The towed Howitzer M1 served on with the US and British armies until the late 1960s, by which time all ammunition stocks had been consumed.

Specification

Calibre:	240mm	9.45in
Length of piece:	8,407mm	331in
Weight travelling:	44,825kg	98,820lb
Weight in action:	29,348kg	64,700lb
Traverse:	45°	
Elevation, firing:	+15 to +65°	
Muzzle velocity (max);	701m/s	2,300ft/sec
Max range:	23,065m	25,225yd
Shell weight:	163.3kg	360lb

An emplaced 240mm Howitzer M1, the figures providing scale

The two main travelling loads of the 240mm Howitzer M1

The barrel section of the 36in (914mm) Little David at Aberdeen Proving Ground

The massive weapon that was to be the largest-calibre artillery piece of the World War II years was originally not an artillery piece but a mortar-pattern device for delivering aircraft bombs against test and proving-ground targets with reasonable accuracy, and at varying velocities. The large calibre, 914mm (36in), had to be introduced in order to cater for the ever-growing size and weight of aircraft bombs. During early 1944, with the invasion of mainland Japan in the early planning stages, questions were raised as to how existing artillery pieces could neutralise the heavy fortifications known to be on the mainland. Some bright spark proposed that the 914mm (36in) bomb-proving device, the Bomb Testing Device T1, could be converted to provide the necessary capability, and from then on the so-called 'Little David' programme acquired a life of its own. The programme involved the development of a strangely shaped projectile with a hemispherical base and a long conical ogive, but even stranger was its weight. This was no less than 1,678.3kg (3,700lb), of which 725kg (1,600lb) was high-explosive, more than sufficient to demolish any structure.

For the howitzer itself, a 7.79-calibre rifled barrel was devised to be placed on trunnions on what was little more than a large steel box dug into the ground. The trunnions were at ground level, with the traversing arc extended from the base of the barrel. The barrel therefore had to be muzzle-loaded, after which the barrel was elevated to ensure the projectile moved down onto the propelling charge at the base of the barrel under the force of gravity. For transport a heavy truck-tractor towed the barrel using a special limber at the rear (muzzle) end. The steel box mounting was placed on detachable wheels for towing by another heavy tractor. Firing tests began at Aberdeen Proving Ground, Maryland, in April 1945. Accuracy proved to be poor and the shock and recoil stresses produced on firing were horrendous, leading to a need to revise the box mounting. When the war ended, technical discussions and investigations were still in progress, meaning that Little David was still at Aberdeen. It never left there. With the war over, there was no longer any need for the device, so, during 1946 the entire project was terminated, leaving the sole example of Little David as an impressive museum piece. Why such an impractical piece of super-heavy artillery was expected to become a viable weapon remains a mystery.

The real weapon, the odd-shaped projectile for the Little David – they are not fins at the base but a display stand

Specification		
Calibre:	914mm	36in
Length of piece:	7,123mm	280.44in
Weight travelling:	not found recorded	
Weight in action:	82,809kg	182,560lb
Traverse:	26°	
Elevation, firing:	+45 to +65°	
Muzzle velocity (max):	not found recorded	
Max range:	8,689m	9,500yd
Shell weight:	1,678.3kg	3,700lb

USSR
107mm Field Gun Model 1910/30

During the 1900s Schneider et Cie of France made a considerable investment in the Putilov Arsenal at St Petersburg. They immediately became very interested in an advanced 107mm (4.2in) gun under development by Putilov at that time. They became so impressed that they eventually brought out a 105mm (4.14in) version and sold it to the French army as the Canon de 105 mle 1913, while the original Russian version was ordered for the Tsarist army to equip Corps-level artillery batteries as the 107mm Field Gun Model 1910 (Pushka obr 1910). Large numbers were manufactured from 1910 to 1917, while some sporadic production carried on into the 1920s. By 1930 sufficient industrial facilities had been re-established in the USSR to undertake a modernisation programme for all Red Army equipment, including the artillery. As an easy option it was decided to modernise the 107mm Model 1910 by installing a new 38-calibre barrel onto the box trail carriage, and some other, less drastic modifications. The gun remained horse-drawn as before, although a few were provided with steel disc wheels for motorised traction.

The result was the 107mm Field Gun Model 1910/30, all earlier versions being brought up to the new standard, providing a maximum range of 16,350m (17,887yd), albeit with a rather limited payload-capacity projectile weighing 17.18kg (37.9lb). As always, with the Soviet armed forces, the numbers were enormous in contrast to many other armed forces' holdings. Although precise figures are not available, the totals ran into thousands. During the early phases of Operation Barbarossa the German army captured hundreds and almost immediately turned them against their former owners. As vast stockpiles of 107mm ammunition had been captured, the Model 1910/30 became an established German weapon as the 10.7cm K 352(r), most serving on the Eastern Front with the rest being incorporated into the Atlantic Wall defences.

During the late 1930s there were plans to replace the Model 1910/30 with a completely redesigned

The 107mm Field Gun Model 1940 M60, destined never to be produced In quantity, thanks to the German invasion of 1941

Model 1940, also referred to as the M60, with a split-trail carriage and a barrel lengthened to 43.5 calibres. Almost as soon as Model 1940 production started, the Germans invaded and the production line was destroyed. Soviet planners subsequently decided to concentrate on heavier and more effective Corps-level artillery calibres, so no further production ensued. Plans to place a suitably modified variant of the Model 1940 in KV-1 and IS-1 heavy tank turrets therefore had to be abandoned.

Specification		
Calibre:	106.7mm	4.2in
Length of piece:	4,054mm	159in
Weight travelling:	2,580kg	5,689lb
Weight in action:	2,380kg	5,248lb
Traverse:	6°	
Elevation, firing:	-5 to +37°	
Muzzle velocity (max):	670m/s	2,198ft/sec
Max range:	16,350m	17,887yd
Shell weight:	17.18kg	37.9lb

The 107mm Field Gun Model 1910/30

By the late 1920s much of the Soviet artillery park was ancient to the point of embarrassment, as the bulk of the artillery park dated back to the early 1900s, if not before. As the post-civil-war period was one of national upheaval on a grand scale, there was little chance to rectify matters until the nation's heavy industrial infrastructure could be rebuilt, but by about 1930 things were becoming established to the point where artillery production could recommence on the required scale. One of the results was a 122mm (4.8in) gun barrel 46.3 calibres long placed on an already existing carriage, that of the 152mm (6in) Gun Howitzer Model 1910/34 (qv). This 122mm model could fire a 25kg (55.125lb) high-explosive projectile (known to the Soviets as HE-FRAG (high-explosive fragmentation)) to 8,940m (9,780yd). The result became the 122mm Field Gun Model 1931. Installing new guns on existing carriages, or new carriages being used to carrying existing barrels, became a standard practice among Soviet artillery design bureaus. From about 1930 onwards it was unusual to find an entirely new Soviet ordnance-and-carriage combination.

With the Model 1931 the new barrel (ordnance designation A-19) was placed on a split-trail carriage that gave the barrel a wide angle of traverse, even then (the early 1930s) deemed essential for anti-tank warfare, where every piece of Soviet artillery, no matter what the calibre, was expected to be employed as an anti-tank gun when the opportunity arose. The Model 1931 also displayed all the other features that Soviet design bureaux were to follow. While the end result was

entirely adequate in every respect, from range and projectile weight to handling and ease of use, the overall impression was of great strength and no frills or unnecessary refinements. The strength factor was introduced to cater for the rough terrain and equally rough handling they were expected to endure. The lack of refinement came from the Soviet philosophy that artillery was regarded as an expendable commodity in war, so there was no need to lavish fine finishes or other niceties on items that were expected to be lost.

So many Model 1931s were captured by the Germans from 1941 onwards that the Model 1931 became part of the German armoury as the 12.2cm K 390/1(r); Finland received 29. Most were retained for front-line operations on the Eastern Front, while others were incorporated into the Atlantic Wall defences.

Specification		
Calibre:	121.92mm	4.8in
Length of piece:	5,650mm	222.44in
Weight travelling:	7,800kg	17,200lb
Weight in action:	7,100kg	15,656lb
Traverse:	56°	
Elevation, firing:	-4 to +45°	
Muzzle velocity (max):	800m/s	2,625ft/sec
Max range:	20,870m	22,832yd
Shell weight:	25kg	55.125lb

The 122mm Field Gun Model 1931/37 (A-19)

When the carriage of the 152mm Gun-Howitzer Model 1937 (qv) was being manufactured it became apparent that production of the gun barrels was going to be delayed. In order to build up numbers and replace at least some of the antiques still in the Soviet inventory, it was decided to place the 122mm (4.8in) 46.3-calibre gun barrel used for the Model 1931 onto the new gun-howitzer carriage. The result became the 122mm Field Gun Model 1931/37, the A-19 ordnance designation being retained.

In appearance the 122mm Model 1931 and Model 1931/37 appeared to be identical, apart from the prominent equilibrator horns sticking up on each side of the barrel. On the Model 1931 they sloped forward. To enable the original barrel to be installed on the new carriage some modifications affecting the balancing had to be introduced, resulting in the equilibrator horns sloping towards the rear. The new carriage introduced a marginally wider traverse and an increase in elevation to +65°, but the ballistic performance remained as for the original Model 1931 gun. As with the Model 1931, the Model 1931/37 was towed with the trails lifted onto a limber, by either horses or trucks. It seems, although it cannot be certain, that once the Model 1931/37 hybrid entered production, that of the Model 1931 was diverted to conversion to the 152mm (6in) Gun-Howitzer Model 1910/34 (qv). By 1941 the

A 122mm Field Gun Model 1931/37 (A-19) ready to move

ammunition suite had grown from the original HE-FRAG to include smoke, illuminating and other projectile natures.

German records regarding the numerous Model 1931/37s captured from 1941 onwards make little distinct mention of the 12.2cm K 390/2(r), as the Model 1931/37 officially became known, noting that 424 were impressed into German service. More were handed out as political 'gifts' to neutral Spain in an attempt to maintain good relations. A total of 200 examples of the German booty ended up in the Atlantic Wall (128) and other coastal defences around occupied Europe and the Mediterranean. The problem is that these totals collectively relate just to the general term of 12.2cm K 390(r), so part of the total must include the Model 1931. By March 1944 the K 390(r) total is given as 224, reflecting combat losses, while as late as March 1945 there were still nearly 200,000 captured projectiles in German

stockpiles. Back in the Soviet Union a modified model of the Model 1931 gun, known as the A-19S, was used as the main armament of the SU-122, a self-propelled assault gun mounted in an armoured superstructure on a KV heavy tank chassis. Production of the towed Model 1931/37 had reached 2,926 examples by 1946. Production then ceased.

Specification		
Calibre:	121.92mm	4.8in
Length of piece:	5,650mm	222.44in
Weight travelling:	7,907kg	17,435lb
Weight in action:	7,117kg	15,663lb
Traverse:	58°	
Elevation, firing:	-2 to +65°	
Muzzle velocity (max):	800m/s	2,625ft/sec
Max range:	20,870m	22,832yd
Shell weight:	25kg	55.125lb

USSR
152mm Field Gun Model 1910/30

The barrel of a 152mm Field Gun Model 1910/30 on its special transporter

Many results emerged from the pre-1910 association between Schneider et Cie of France and the Putilov Arsenal at St Petersburg. One was a great deal of modernisation of the Putilov production methods and machinery, while another was the importing of various items of then-modern Schneider designs, some of which were eventually licence-produced in Russia. Into the latter category came a Schneider 152mm (6in) gun, licence-produced as the 152mm Field Gun Model 1910. It was originally a Schneider export product, one of several models sold

to Russia, as the French army saw no use for such a gun at that time. The Model 1910 soldiered on in some numbers until 1930, when it was decided to add the piece to the modernisation list. After due modification it then became the Model 1910/30, or 152-10/30.

Some changes were introduced to the rather complicated and bulky carriage, while the modernised ordnance was given a new liner and a muzzle brake was added. The revised barrel length with the muzzle brake was 32 calibres. The result was a virtually new gun with a useful service-life extension, but some unwelcome aspects of the original design remained. There were two models: one with steel wheels for towing by horse teams, and one with rubber tyres for mechanical traction. In both forms any long moves involved breaking the gun and carriage down into four loads, with the resultant extended time needed to get the gun into action once at a selected firing site. The rubber-tyred-wheel model could be towed in two loads, but only for short distances and over good surfaces.

The number of 152mm Model 1910/30 conversions made has not yet been found recorded, but it must have been significant, as the gun had to form a stopgap until more modern equipments appeared. As such it had a commendable ballistic performance. It could fire a 43.56kg (96.05lb) projectile to 16,800m (18,380yd), but the slow times in and out of action cannot have made the Model 1910/30 a popular gun. The rate of fire was also rather slow, at from two to three rounds a minute (at best). It seems that the type was already being phased out of service when the Germans invaded in 1941. They allotted the designation 15.2cm K 483(r) to the Model 1910/30, but no records have yet been found of them in German service, not even among the artillery-hungry Atlantic Wall defences.

Specification		
Calibre:	152.4mm	6in
Length of piece:	4,855mm	191.16in
Weight travelling:	7,908kg	17,435lb
Weight in action:	6,700kg	14,773lb
Traverse:	4.5°	
Elevation, firing:	-7 to +37°	
Muzzle velocity (max):	650m/s	2,133ft/sec
Max range:	16,800m	18,380yd
Shell weight:	43.56kg	96.05lb

USSR
152mm Gun B-10

Hiding under a tree is this elusive 152mm Gun B-10

The 152mm (6in) Gun B-10 (152-55) is one of the mysteries of the Soviet ordnance scene. It has been referred to as the Model 1935, while some references mention a Model 1931. There was also a 152mm B-30. The B-10 appears to have been developed from 1929 onwards, at about the same time as the 203mm (8in) Model 1931 howitzer (qv), and shared much the same tractor-based tracked carriage. Some references mention this gun having been developed for the long-range, counter-battery role. It appears that the 152mm B-10 ordnance may have been based on a naval or coastal defence gun, as the ammunition weights involved do not tally with any other Soviet-era land campaign weapon.

The gun travelled with its two trail legs joined together on a wheeled limber. The trails remained side by side when the gun was emplaced, a projectile-loading trolley travelling along two rails to assist the loading process into the breech with its interrupted-screw block. Each trail leg had an oversize trail spade, indicating that the recoil forces must have been considerable. The usual towing vehicle was a 'Voroshilovets' heavy tracked tractor with the gun crew seated on benches in an open area at the rear; two of the crew travelled on seats either side of the barrel. Despite the twin trail legs, on-carriage traverse was limited to only 8°.

Just about all the accessible details available regarding this odd gun are contained in this summary but, despite doubts in some quarters, it certainly existed. A German intelligence document, dated September 1943, mentions it in sparse detail and, the clincher, an example can be seen at the Sevastopol War Memorial museum. What is known is that it fired a 48.58kg (107lb) projectile to 27,000m (29,540yd) – one reference mentions 26,000m (28,435yd) – using a two-part propelling charge system. Even here doubts arise, for another reference mentions a 43.5kg (95.9lb) projectile being fired to 29,755m (32,540yd) at a muzzle

velocity of 940 m/s (3,084ft/sec). Not even the barrel length is certain. One German reference mentions 50 calibres, while another, the Soviet designation (152-55), indicates 55 calibres. For their purposes the Germans listed the 152mm Gun B-10 as the 15.2cm K 440(r) but no reference can be found to any in German service, which may be significant. It remains one of the most elusive of all Soviet guns – it cannot have been produced in anything other than small numbers.

Specification		
Calibre:	152.4mm	6in
Length of piece:	7,620mm	300in
Weight travelling:	not found recorded	
Weight in action:	18,202kg	40,093lb
Traverse:	8°	
Elevation, firing:	0 to +60°	
Muzzle velocity (max):	880m/s	2,887ft/sec
Max range:	27,000m	29,540yd
Shell weight:	48.58kg	107lb

USSR
122mm Field Howitzer Model 1910/30

Yet another result of the association between the Putilov Arsenal and Schneider et Cie of France was a Schneider export model 122mm (4.8in) howitzer that was adopted by the Tsarist army as the 122mm Field Howitzer Model 1910, or 10S. It was licence-produced by Putilov in some numbers, so it became one of the mainstays of the old Tsarist army from 1914 to 1917. Thereafter the type remained in

service with the new Soviet army until 1930, when the type became the subject of not so much a modernisation programme, but a major renovation programme.

While the original stubby 12.8-calibre barrel was retained, it was relined and the chamber was enlarged to accommodate heavier propellant charges, increasing the muzzle velocity and

therefore potential range. Virtually every part of the box-trail carriage was brought back to an as-new condition and strengthened where necessary to withstand the extra recoil forces produced by the increased charges. The end result was the 122mm Field Howitzer Model 1910/30 with a range increased to 8,940m (9,780yd) firing a 21.76kg (47.987lb) projectile.

The Model 1910/30 thus formed a useful stopgap until more modern equipments became available, but it had its shortcomings. These were mainly due to the limitations of the box trail carriage. Traverse was severely restricted to a total of only 4.7°, far too limited for gunners' comfort, as it meant that even the smallest target switches involved manhandling the entire howitzer and relaying it. As the howitzer was originally intended to be horse-drawn, the original Model 1910 wooden-spoked wheels were retained. By 1940 some of the Model 1910/30 howitzers had been transferred to mechanised traction in order to keep up with motorised infantry and other formations.

By then the Model 1910/30 was regarded as the overdue-for-replacement anachronism it

undoubtedly was, so there was little point in modifying the wheels. Any truck-drawn moves therefore had to be made at slow speeds, the end of the carriage suspended on a limber. This inability to move fast was no doubt one reason why so many Model 1910/30s fell into German hands during 1941 and after. One listing mentions 917 examples being transferred to German service as the 12.2cm leFH 388(r). Most of these were retained for service on the Eastern Front but at least 23 were assigned to coastal defence duties. A batch was also sent to Finland.

Specification		
Calibre:	121.92mm	4.8in
Length of piece:	1,561mm	61.5in
Weight travelling:	2,530kg	5,579lb
Weight in action:	1,466kg	3,231lb
Traverse:	4.7°	
Elevation, firing:	-3 to +43°	
Muzzle velocity (max):	364m/s	1,194ft/sec
Max range:	8,940m	9,780yd
Shell weight:	21.76kg	47.987lb

USSR
122mm Field Howitzer Model 1938

One of the greatest artillery success stories of the Great Patriotic War years was the 122mm (4.8in) Field Howitzer Model 1938 (M-30), or 122-38. Unlike many other Soviet artillery equipments of the time, the Model 1938 had a completely new barrel and carriage combination, although it continued to fire the same projectiles as the 122mm Model 1910/30 howitzer it was designed to replace. The first examples were

delivered to the Soviet armed forces during late 1938. The Model 1938 immediately became regarded as one of the best howitzers in its class in service anywhere. The overall construction was light but sturdy, a 22.7-calibre barrel resting on a split-trail carriage with solid rubber-tyred, steel disc wheels, as nothing other than mechanised traction was likely to be employed. Maximum range was 11,800m (12,909yd).

One of the most successful artillery designs of the World War II period, the 122mm Field Howitzer Model 1938

Mass production did not commence properly until 1940 and continued in the USSR until 1955, by which time the production total had reached 19,266. That total is a reflection of how important the Model 1938 was to the Soviet armed forces. It became their standard field howitzer, playing a significant part in the massed artillery barrages that came to epitomise the Soviet way of conducting war. One important fact throughout the history of the Model 1938 is that it remained unchanged from the first production example until the last. Post-war nations, such as Bulgaria, may have introduced pneumatic tyres, but that was an exception. New ammunition natures were gradually introduced, including a shaped-charge anti-tank projectile.

Large numbers of the Model 1938 inevitably fell into German hands to become the 12.2cm sFH 396(r). They became a standard German weapon on the Eastern Front, as the Germans captured massive stocks of 122mm ammunition. As late as March 1945 the Germans still held 286,500 122mm projectiles ready to be fired. Some of the captured howitzers were sent to Finland, while others, again inevitably, ended up in coastal defence installations.

Back in the Soviet Union the ordnance of the Model 1938 was adapted to be the main armament of the SU-122 assault howitzer, built into an armoured superstructure on a T-34 medium tank chassis. One indication of the overall success of the Model 1938 is that it remains in service all around the world during the 21st century, including with nations outside the old Warsaw Pact. It even remains in production in China, where it is marketed as the 122mm Type 54-1, suitable ammunition remaining available from numerous production sources.

Specification		
Calibre:	121.92mm	4.8in
Length of piece:	2,800mm	110.25in
Weight travelling:	2,800kg	6,173lb
Weight in action:	2,450kg	5,400lb
Traverse:	49°	
Elevation, firing:	-3 to +63.5°	
Muzzle velocity (max):	515m/s	1,690ft/sec
Max range:	11,800m	12,909yd
Shell weight:	21.76kg	47.98lb

122mm Field Howitzer Model 1938

The 152mm (6in) Field Howitzer Model 1903/30, or 152-09/30, was yet another elderly piece that owed its survival until 1941 to a 1930 upgrade programme. It was originally manufactured at the Putilov Arsenal, St Petersburg, and by the Perm artillery plant. Although often credited as a Putilov design it almost certainly had a great deal of French Schneider influence incorporated, if not a full licence-manufacturing agreement. The original horse-drawn Model 1909 was a sound but unremarkable howitzer of completely conventional design, with a box trail and short barrel. They soldiered on in an unremarkable fashion throughout the Great War and Civil War years and after. It appears that the type was kept in sporadic and limited production throughout the 1920s, so enough were on hand during the late 1920s for the Model 1909 to be considered for a modernisation upgrade. This resulted in the 152mm Field Howitzer Model 1903/30l.

For this weapon the modernisation changes were few, and mainly involved the barrel being replaced by a renovated 14-calibre component, and a few corresponding carriage changes. No provision was made for mechanised traction, the original wooden-spoked wheels being retained, along with the shield. To make the towed load better balanced during moves, the barrel could be disconnected from the recoil mechanism and drawn back over the box trail. The new barrel could fire a 40kg (88.2lb) projectile to 9,854m (10,780yd). It appears that updated ammunition was introduced at about the same time, including a four-part propellant charge system.

By any standards, significant numbers of these equipments were modernised from 1931 onwards (2,030 by the time the Germans invaded), although the programme had a relatively low priority. Out of this total 14 were sold to Finland. By 1941, when the Germans invaded the Soviet Union, examples still in Soviet service had been relegated to second-line, reserve and training duties. Despite their age and limited all-round performance, they still became grist to the German mill, for they appear under their new designation of 15.2cm sFH 445(r) on lists of coastal defence weapons, even though it seems they did not last in that role for long. A gradual transfer of captured Model 1909/30s to Finland took place from 1941 onwards, resulting of a total of 109 Finnish equipments by June 1944. Those Finnish howitzers remained in local service until the mid-1960s.

Specification		
Calibre:	152.4mm	6in
Length of piece:	2,160mm	85in
Weight travelling:	3,050kg	6,725lb
Weight in action:	2,275kg	6,008lb
Traverse:	5.7°	
Elevation, firing:	0 to +41°	
Muzzle velocity (max):	391m/s	1,283ft/sec
Max range:	9,854m	10,780yd
Shell weight:	40kg	88.2lb

152mm Field Howitzer Model 1903/30

USSR
152mm Field Howitzer Model 1910/30

A 152mm Field Howitzer Model 1910/30

The original 152mm Field Howitzer Model 1910 was the howitzer that gave rise to the successful French Canon de 155 C mle 1917 Schneider (qv). It was a Schneider commercial product, unwanted by the French army of the period up to 1915 but, in 152mm (6in) form it attracted the attentions of the Tsarist army. They purchased a licence-manufacturing agreement for the type to be built, not at the usual Putilov Arsenal, but at the Perm artillery plant. The numbers manufactured remain inaccessible, but must have been significant because the Model 1910 proved itself to be an excellent and reliable field howitzer, firing the same ammunition as the 152mm Model 1909. As with the Model 1909, the Model 1910 was selected for modernisation from about 1927 onwards. Nothing could be implemented until about 1931, when the programme reached the hardware stage.

With the Model 1910 the changes made were few, being limited to an all-round renovation process for both the 12-calibre barrel and carriage. The main alteration was to the wheels. They were changed to the steel disc type with rubber tyres. Together with some modifications to the wheel bearings and brakes, these changes rendered the Model 1910 suitable for motorised traction and it then became the 152mm Field Howitzer Model 1910/30. (Some references mention the 152mm Model 1910/37). The limber wheels were also altered to the new pattern so during moves the M1910/30 could then be towed in a single load at relatively high speeds. There was no longer any need for the barrel to be drawn back over the box-trail carriage, as was the case when horses were involved.

By the time the Germans invaded in 1941, the Model 1910/30 had followed the same path as the Model 1909/30, namely to second-line, reserve and training duties, although they were soon sent to the front lines, where many were lost, either due to enemy action or capture. The Germans gave the Model 1910/30 the designation of 15.2cm sFH 446(r). Having captured significant numbers, they apparently found them unsuitable for retention, probably due to their non-standard calibre compared to the other C 17 S booty, which was in 155mm (6.1in). It appears that captured Model 1910/30s were therefore scrapped. (A small number of the original Model 1910 howitzers (nine) were acquired in 1918 by Finland, where they remained operational until the 1960s.)

Specification		
Calibre:	152.4mm	6in
Length of piece:	1,830mm	72in
Weight travelling:	3,230kg	7,122lb
Weight in action:	2,580kg	5,680lb
Traverse:	4.8°	
Elevation, firing:	-6.7 to +39.75°	
Muzzle velocity (max):	391m/s	1,283ft/sec
Max range:	9,854m	10,780yd
Shell weight:	40kg	88.2lb

USSR
152mm Gun-Howitzer Model 1910/34

By the mid-1930s, Soviet artillery planners were viewing the future with some trepidation because, in spite of their rapid upgrading measures involving existing equipments, it was becoming apparent that they were in danger of being outperformed by artillery developments elsewhere, especially from Germany. This realisation formed the background to a series of hasty measures

German recognition illustration of a 152mm Gun-Howitzer Model 1910/34

introduced during an attempt to rectify the situation in numerical, if not in all-round, performance terms. One such measure was initiated by placing the new muzzle-braked ordnance intended for the 152mm (6in) Gun-Howitzer Model 1937 (qv) onto the readily available split-trail carriage of the 122mm (4.8in) Field Gun Model 1931 A-19 (also qv). At the same time a small shield was added, as usual in Soviet practice to protect the gun mechanisms, rather than the crew, from damage. The result was the 152mm Gun-Howitzer Model 1910/34 or 152-10/34. This hybrid combination was termed a gun-howitzer because the long, 29-calibre barrel provided something approaching the range performance of a comparable gun while retaining the flexible and economic bagged propellant system of a howitzer.

The Model 1910/34 had a maximum range of 17,600m (19,254yd) firing the 43.56kg (96.05lb) high-explosive fragmentation (HE-FRAG) projectile that remains the standard 152mm projectile to this day. The gun-howitzer format was thereafter widely adopted throughout the artillery world, where it is now rare to find a new design of dedicated gun or howitzer. As with so many of the other Soviet hybrid improvisations of the era, the 152mm Model 1910/34 was intended to be a stopgap until something better came along. In the event, in order to somehow improve the numbers of relatively modern artillery equipments in service, the number

of conversions ran into the thousands, the type first seeing action during the Finno-Soviet Winter War of 1939–40.

By the time the Germans invaded the Soviet Union in 1941 the Model 1910/34 was in service in large numbers, only for the bulk of them to fall into German hands as the 15.2cm K 433/2(r). With them came so much ammunition that the Germans acquired sufficient to last them until 1943, when series production of 152mm ammunition began in Germany. Some of this 'German' ammunition was destined to be also fired from the Model 1937 howitzer (see following entry), which the Germans preferred over the Model 1910/34. Some Model 1910/34s ended up in Finland, while others were handed out to nations sympathetic to the German cause, such as Slovakia.

Specification		
Calibre:	152.4mm	6in
Length of piece:	4,404mm	173.4in
Weight travelling:	7,820kg	17,243lb
Weight in action:	7,100kg	15,655lb
Traverse:	58°	
Elevation, firing:	-4 to +45°	
Muzzle velocity (max):	650m/s	2,113ft/sec
Max range:	17,600m	19,254yd
Shell weight:	43.56kg	96.05lb

USSR
152mm Gun-Howitzer Model 1937 (ML-20)

The gun-howitzer that was to become one of the most important items of Soviet artillery during the Great Patriotic War years was another hybrid. This time it was produced by an alliance of the new gun-howitzer of the 152mm (6in) Model 1937

(ML-20) and the increased-elevation, split-trail carriage of the 122mm Field Gun Model 1931/37 (qv). The new combination became the 152mm Gun-Howitzer Model 1937 (ML-20), or 152-37.

It was manufactured in two forms: one had spoked

A 152mm Gun-Howitzer Model 1937 (ML-20) ready to move

wheels for horse traction, the other, for motorised traction, had double-tyred steel wheels. Both were manufactured in huge numbers, often under difficult conditions, from 1937 onwards. One reference states the total by 1946 (when production ceased) as 13,019 units, which indicates the importance of the Model 1937 to the Soviet armed forces. It became the backbone of the Soviet artillery arm, forming the bulk of the gun-howitzers that delivered the massive barrages employed until the Fall of Berlin.

In ballistic terms the Model 1937 could fire the standard 152mm 43.56kg (96.05lb) HE-FRAG projectile to 17,265m (18,888yd). In addition to its field artillery value it was often employed as an anti-tank gun, as with all other Soviet artillery pieces, relying on projectile weight and its explosive payload for its anti-armour effects. The Model 37 ordnance was modified into ML-20S form for installation in two self-propelled assault-gun models. One was the SU-152, carried on a KV heavy tank chassis, and the other the ISU-153, on the JS heavy tank chassis.

Returning to the towed form, the Model 1937 also became an important increment within the German gun park after 1941. At one time the German army had captured at least 974 Model 1937s along with masses of ammunition. As outlined, some of this ammunition was shared with the Model 1910/34 (see previous entry). The Germans used the Model 1937 as the 15.2cm KH 433/1(r). That designation appears on many German documents, including lists of coastal defence guns. At least 217 units were diverted to the coastal defence role at locations as far apart as Italy and Denmark. Sixty-eight of them were sent to the Balkans to defend various naval bases, while 118 ended up at various locations along the Atlantic Wall. After 1945 the Model 1937 was distributed among the Warsaw Pact nations, some of them serving on until at least the early 1990s.

Specification		
Calibre:	152.4mm	6in
Length of piece:	4,404mm	173.4in
Weight travelling:	7,930kg	17,485lb
Weight in action:	7,128kg	15,715lb
Traverse:	58°	
Elevation, firing:	-2 to +65°	
Muzzle velocity:	650m/s	2,113ft/sec
Max range:	17,265m	18,888yd
Shell weight:	43.56kg	96.05lb

A 152mm Gun-Howitzer Model 1937 (ML-20) serving as a coastal defence weapon

USSR
152mm Field Howitzer Model 1938 (M-10)

A German recognition illustration of a 152mm Field Howitzer Model 1938 (M-10)

With the 152mm Field Howitzer Model 1938 (M-10), also known as the 152-38, the Soviet design process of combining existing and new components was carried to an extreme. This time it was a new 152mm (6in) howitzer barrel mounted on the split-trail carriage originally intended for the 107mm (4.2in) Field Gun Model 1940 M60. The 107mm gun model was only just entering production when the Germans invaded during mid-1941 (development appears to have been delayed for ballistic technical reasons). Plans for series production elsewhere were abandoned in favour of heavier-calibre pieces.

The main difference between the gun and howitzer carriages was that the 152mm howitzer had two rubber-tyred wheels on each side whereas the gun had only one. A towing limber also had rubber tyres, and a commonly employed tracked tractor was the 8-tonne capacity 'Komintern' model. In addition, a shield, optional for the gun, seems to have been a fixture on the larger howitzer, although, as usual, mainly to protect the gun mechanisms rather than the crew. The Model 1938 could fire a 43.56kg (96.05lb) HE-FRAG projectile to 12,400m

A 152mm Field Howitzer Model 1938 (M-10)

(13,565m). The maximum rate of fire was four rounds a minute, although sustained fire missions lowered the rate to two a minute, at best.

Production of the 152mm Howitzer Model 1938 began at Artillery Plant No. 172 in late 1939, much earlier than for the 107mm gun, but production was destined not to last as long as had originally been planned. The Model 1938 production line was another casualty of the German invasion of 1941, by which time 1,522 had been manufactured. Production was not resumed elsewhere.

The addition of the 152mm Model 1938 to the relatively modern sector of the Soviet armoury made it one of their more important artillery equipments during the early Great Patriotic War years. It also meant that many of them were captured or destroyed during those early years, perhaps as many as 1,000, in varying states of repair, being lost to the Germans. As the 15.2cm sFH 443(r) the Model 1938 went on to became a major item of equipment for the German army, most of the captured equipments being directed against their former owners as field artillery until they once again became battle casualties or the locally held captured ammunition stocks were consumed. Only three sFH 443(r) equipments have been noted as being diverted to coastal defence, probably in the Baltic region.

Specification		
Calibre:	152.4mm	6in
Length of piece:	3,700mm	145.7in
Weight travelling:	4,550kg	10,033lb
Weight in action:	4,150kg	9,150lb
Traverse:	50°	
Elevation, firing:	-1 to +65°	
Muzzle velocity (max):	508m/s	1,667ft/sec
Max range:	12,400m	13,565yd
Shell weight:	43.56kg	96.05lb

USSR
152mm Field Howitzer Model 1943 (D-1)

Light but still lethal, the 152mm Field Howitzer Model 1943 (D-1)

The initially bewildering array of Soviet artillery guns and howitzers involving various barrel and carriage alliances was enlarged yet further with the 152mm (6in) Field Howitzer Model 1943 (D-1). It was an alliance of the 152mm Model 1938 howitzer barrel (see previous entry) and the 122mm (4.8in) Field Howitzer Model 1938 (qv) carriage and recoil system. Both the carriage and the recoil mechanism were strengthened, while the howitzer barrel acquired a large, double-baffle muzzle brake. The task of marrying the two equipments was carried out by the F. F. Petrov design bureau at the Artillery Plant No. 9 in Sverdlovsk. Production began in August 1943, again at Sverdlovsk, with the intention of replacing the 152mm Field Howitzer Model 1938. The new howitzer, the 152mm Field Howitzer Model 1943 (D-1), remained in production until 1949, by which time the production total had reached 2,827 units.

The main advantage gained by the Model 1943, apart from making use of readily available equipments, was that the relatively light 122mm howitzer carriage made the 152mm Model 1943 much lighter and easier to handle than the earlier 152mm Howitzer Model 1938 while remaining just as stable and using the same ammunition. It could therefore fire a 43.51kg (95.91lb) OF-530 HE-FRAG projectile (developed for the Model 1943) to a creditable 12,400m (13,565m). The lower weight also meant that the Model 1943 could be economically towed by a suitable truck rather than a specialised artillery tractor, while, once in action, it

was much easier and quicker to switch the barrel from one target to another. As usual, the Model 1943 was also intended to be employed as an anti-tank weapon when necessary, initially relying mainly on projectile weight for its anti-armour performance, although specialised anti-armour projectiles were introduced later.

The Model 1943 never did manage to replace all other Soviet 152mm howitzers by the time the Great Patriotic War ended, but it did so after 1945. When it was replaced in its turn, the Model 1943 was also handed on to various Warsaw Pact states. With time it was gradually relegated to becoming part of Soviet military aid to nations all around the world, so it may still be encountered to this day in some parts of the globe. During the war years the Model 1943 arrived too late to make much impression on the German armoury, as by the time it was fielded the German army was only rarely in a position to capture Soviet equipment on any scale.

Specification		
Calibre:	152.4mm	6in
Length of piece:	3,749mm	147.6in
Weight travelling:	3,635kg	8,008lb
Weight in action:	3,601kg	7,940lb
Traverse:	35°	
Elevation, firing:	-3 to +63.5°	
Muzzle velocity (max):	508m/s	1,667ft/sec
Max range:	12,400m	13,565yd
Shell weight:	43.51kg	95.91lb

USSR
203mm Howitzer Model 1931 (B-4)

With the 203mm (8in) Howitzer Model 1931 (B-4) we come to the top calibre of the Soviet heavy artillery of the Great Patriotic War. Heavier-calibre equipments did exist within the Soviet arsenal after 1941 but they were either railway, coast or experimental equipments, some of them imported. The 203mm Howitzer Model 1931 (B-4) was unusual in several ways, not the least being that the carriage rode on tractor-type tracks. Another item of note was the number of sub-variants that might be encountered. There were at least six, all of them contained within the Model 1931 designation. Firstly, there were two barrel-lengths: 22 calibres and 25 calibres. Then there were three types of suspension. The main one, as already mentioned, employed tractor tracks, but there were two others. One had large solid-steel traction engine-pattern wheels and the other had much smaller two-wheeled bogies. Howitzers of both lengths might be encountered on any one of these three suspension types.

Most of these variations seem to have been introduced during the early production stages. The 25-calibre-barrel model with the tracked suspension appears to have been the most numerous (the data provided refers to this version), other equipments no doubt being gradually retrofitted to the same standard. The only thing all the sub-variants had in common was that the howitzer travelled in two loads, barrel and carriage.

Development of the Model 1931 began during the late 1920s, with production not commencing until 1937. Production ceased during 1941, no doubt to concentrate on less cumbersome equipments. By then 889 units had been manufactured. They served on the Eastern Front only, captured examples falling into German hands becoming the 20.3cm H 503(r).

Getting the Howitzer Model 1931 in and out of action was a laborious process, as once the barrel was mated with the box trail, heavy trail spades had to be dug into the ground to form recoil anchors, while two heavy, tensioned, ground cables were

A 203mm Howitzer Model 1931 (B-4) on show

added to the rear on each side, plus another to the front, all secured by steel pickets and all to keep the howitzer under control during firing, although limiting barrel traverse.

The Model 1931 proved to be a fearsome weapon, especially during urban warfare, when it was frequently employed to demolish entire building blocks, such as during the Battle for Berlin in 1945. Small numbers are still retained by the modern Russian army for precisely this purpose.

Specification		
Calibre:	203mm	8in
Length of piece:	5,087mm	200.3in
Weight travelling:	19,000kg	41,887lb
Weight in action:	17,700kg	39,028lb
Traverse:	8°	
Elevation, firing:	0 to +60°	
Muzzle velocity:	607m/s	1,992ft/sec
Max range:	12,400m	13,565yd
Shell weight:	100kg	220.5lb

A 203mm Howitzer Model 1931 (B-4) in the field

Glossary

BL	English	Breech Loading	
C	French	Court	(short)
C	German	Construction	(construction) <Construktionsjahr (year of construction)?>
F	German	Feld	(field)
GP	French	Grand Puissance	(great power)
GP-T	French	Grand Puissance Touzzard	
H	German	Haubitze	(howitzer)
K	German	Kanone	(gun)
L	French	Longue	(long)
Le	German	leichte	(light)
lg	German	langer	(long)?>
M	US	Model	
Mrs	German	Mörser	(mortar)
QF	English	Quick Firing	
S	French	Schneider	
S	German	schwere	(heavy)
SK	German	SchiffsKanone	(naval gun)
VZOR	Czech	Model	
WZOR	Polish	Model	

Index